DOS® 6

Sarah E. Hutchinson
Stacey C. Sawyer
Glen J. Coulthard

THE IRWIN ADVANTAGE SERIES
FOR COMPUTER EDUCATION
◆
IRWIN
Burr Ridge, Illinois
Boston, Massachusetts
Sydney, Australia

©Richard D. Irwin, Inc., 1994

Printed in the United States of America.

ISBN 0-256-15791-X

1 2 3 4 5 6 7 8 9 0 ML 1 0 9 8 7 6 5 4

TABLE OF CONTENTS

SESSION 1: FUNDAMENTALS

SESSION 2: MANAGING YOUR FILES

SESSION 3: WORKING WITH DIRECTORIES

SESSION 4: MANAGING YOUR DISKS

SESSION 5: INCREASING YOUR PRODUCTIVITY

USING THIS GUIDE

This tutorial is one in a series of learning guides that lead you through the most popular microcomputer software programs available. Concepts, skills, and procedures are grouped into session topics and are presented in a logical and structured manner. Commands and procedures are introduced using hands-on examples, and you are encouraged to perform the steps along with the guide. Although you may turn directly to a later session, be aware that some sessions require, or at least assume, that you have completed the previous sessions. For maximum benefit, you should also work through the short answer questions and hands-on exercises appearing at the end of each session.

The exercises and examples in this guide use several standard conventions to indicate menu options, keystroke combinations, and command instructions.

MENU INSTRUCTIONS

In the DOS Shell, all Menu bar options and pull-down menu commands have an underlined or highlighted letter in each option. When you need to execute a command from the Menu bar—the row of menu choices across the top of the screen—the tutorial's instruction line separates the Menu bar option from the command with a comma. For example, the command for quitting the DOS Shell is shown as:

> CHOOSE: File, Exit

This instruction tells you to choose the File option on the Menu bar and then to choose the Exit command from the File pull-down menu. The actual steps for choosing a menu command are discussed later in this session.

KEYSTROKES AND KEYSTROKE COMBINATIONS

When two keys must be pressed together, the tutorial's instruction line shows the keys joined with a plus (+) sign. For example, you execute a command from the DOS Shell Menu bar by holding down the (Alt) key and then pressing the key with the underlined or highlighted letter of the desired command.

To illustrate this type of keystroke combination, the following statement shows how to access the File menu option:

PRESS: (Alt)+f

In this instruction, you press the (Alt) key first and then hold it down while you press the *f* key. Once both keys have been pressed, they are then immediately released.

COMMAND INSTRUCTIONS

This guide indicates with a special typeface data that you are required to type in yourself. For example:

TYPE: `George Washington`

When you are required to enter unique information, such as the current date or your name, the instruction appears in italics. The following instruction directs you to type your name in place of the actual words: "your name."

TYPE: *your name*

Instructions that use general directions rather than a specific option or command name appear italicized in the regular typeface.

SELECT: *a different pattern for the chart*

The Quick Reference sections incorporate "syntax diagrams" which review standard command lines. Optional components of the command are placed in square brackets. Variables that hold specific information appear italicized in the syntax diagram, similar to the following:

Syntax: DIR [*drive:*][*path*][/P][/W]

This instruction shows that the disk drive designation, path, /P, and /W choices are all optional. In other words, you can execute this command by entering DIR and then pressing (Enter). Because the drive and path are italicized, you can also substitute your own drive and path information for these variables.

ADVANTAGE DISKETTE

The Advantage Diskette, provided with this guide or by your instructor, contains the files that you use in each session and in the hands-on exercises. This diskette is extremely important for ensuring the success of the guide.

If you are using this guide in a self-study program, we suggest that you make a copy of the Advantage Diskette using the DOS DISKCOPY command. When the guide asks you to insert the Advantage Diskette, you insert and work with the copied diskette instead. By following this procedure, you will be able to work through the guide again at a later date using a fresh copy of the Advantage Diskette. For more information on using the DISKCOPY command, please refer to your DOS manual.

SESSION 1

DOS 6:
FUNDAMENTALS

A microcomputer operating system is the software program that runs the computer. It is the first program loaded when the computer is turned on, and, without it, you cannot use your word processing software, spreadsheet software, or any other application software programs.

MS-DOS is the most commonly used microcomputer operating system. Understanding DOS will help you to get the most out of your computer. This session gets you started with the basics.

PREVIEW

When you have completed this session, you will be able to:

Explain the purpose of an operating system.
•
Describe the features of DOS 6.
•
Explain the process of booting a computer.
•
Execute several commands from the DOS command line.
•
Load the DOS Shell.
•
Describe the components of the DOS Shell.
•
Access the DOS Shell Help facility.
•
Leave the DOS Shell.

1

Why Is This Session Important?

What Is DOS?

    File Management

    Directory and Disk Management

File- and Disk-Naming Conventions

    File-Naming Conventions

    Disk-Drive-Naming Conventions

Working with DOS

    The Command Line

    The DOS Shell

Internal and External Commands

Loading DOS: The Boot Process

Using the Keyboard

Using the Command Line

    Entering Commands

    Moving from Disk to Disk

    Setting the Clock (DATE and TIME)

    Displaying the DOS Version (VER)

    Displaying a List of Files (DIR)

    Clearing the Screen (CLS)

    Getting Help (HELP)

Working with the DOS Shell

    How the Mouse Is Used

    How the Keyboard Is Used

Using the DOS Shell

    The Guided Tour

    Moving the Selection Cursor

    Menu Bar

    Dialog Boxes

    Getting Help

    Accessing the Command Line

    Exiting the DOS Shell

Summary

    Command Summary

Key Terms

Exercises

    Short Answer

    Hands-On

WHY IS THIS SESSION IMPORTANT?

This guide leads you step-by-step through DOS 6. Whether you are new to computers or new to DOS, this guide provides you with a comprehensive overview of the most popular microcomputer operating system. In each of the following sessions, you will learn commands and procedures for managing the resources of your computer.

In this session, you learn the following DOS commands:

CLS	DOSSHELL	VER
DATE	HELP	
DIR	TIME	

After exploring the basics of file and disk management, this session discusses the conventions for naming files and disk drives, and then summarizes the boot or startup process. You also learn to execute commands using the command line and the DOS Shell, a graphical program which makes managing files and disks easier than ever before.

WHAT IS DOS?

DOS is an abbreviation for Disk Operating System. An **operating system** is a collection of software programs that manage, coordinate, and in a sense bring life to the computer hardware (the physical components of a computer). Every computer must have an operating system to control its basic input and output operations, such as receiving commands from the keyboard (input) and displaying information to the screen (output). An operating system is also responsible for managing the storage areas of a computer, namely hard disks and floppy diskettes.

Without an operating system, you cannot communicate with the computer. When you give the computer a command, the operating system relays your instructions to the brain of the computer, called the microprocessor or CPU. You cannot speak directly to the CPU since it only understands machine language made up of 1s and 0s. If you are working in an application software program, such as WordPerfect or Lotus 1-2-3, commands that you give the application are sent through the operating system to the CPU.

There are several operating systems available for microcomputers, including MS-DOS, PC-DOS, OS/2, Windows NT, UNIX, and System 7 for the Macintosh. Microsoft Windows 3.1 is not an operating system; it is a software program that works with DOS to provide a graphical environment for your computer. Although each operating system has its advantages, the majority of IBM and IBM-compatible microcomputers use MS-DOS or PC-DOS. These two operating systems are almost identical except for their respective producers, Microsoft and IBM. This guide is specifically written for MS-DOS versions 6.0, 6.2, and 6.21, but sections may also be used with MS-DOS 5.0, PC-DOS 5.0, and PC-DOS 6.1.

FILE MANAGEMENT

DOS provides several tools for performing basic file management tasks such as copying, moving, renaming, and deleting files. There are two categories of files that appear on hard disks and floppy diskettes: **program files** and **data files**. Program files consist of computer instructions for performing a certain task or for running an application software program. Data files contain the work that you create using an application, such as a letter or a spreadsheet. You use DOS file management commands to manage both program and data files.

Table 1.1 shows the similarities between a manual and an electronic file management system.

Table 1.1	*Manual System*	*Electronic System*
File Management: Comparison	Place a document in a filing cabinet for permanent storage	Save a document in a disk file for permanent storage
	Use a photocopier to duplicate an important document	Use DOS to copy and back up an important disk file
	Throw away old documents to free up room in the filing cabinet	Use DOS to delete a file from the hard disk or a floppy diskette
	Retrieve a document from the garbage that you mistakenly threw away	Use DOS to undelete a file that was mistakenly erased
	File a document under a new name	Use DOS to rename a file

DIRECTORY AND DISK MANAGEMENT

Directory management refers to the organization of program and data files on a hard disk or a floppy diskette. Hard disks are usually mounted inside the computer, while floppy diskettes are removable and provide far less storage capacity. Because one hard disk can store data that would normally fill several filing cabinets, it is important that you learn how to organize and maintain the files on your disks.

On a new disk there is only one area for storing files, called the **root directory**. Using DOS, you create **subdirectories** underneath the root directory to isolate and store each application's files and your data files. You can also create subdirectories within subdirectories for further classification. The organization of subdirectories on a disk is called a **directory structure** or **directory tree**. Because a floppy diskette has limited capacity, you typically store files in its root directory without worrying about separating them into separate subdirectories. Using the much greater storage capacity on a hard disk requires careful planning.

Think of the root directory as the top of a filing cabinet and each subdirectory as a drawer or folder in the cabinet. Obviously, you could not continually place documents on top of the cabinet without the files reaching the ceiling. One solution would be to move the files from the top of the filing cabinet into the cabinet drawers. On a computer, this activity represents moving files from the root directory of a disk to its subdirectories. A hard disk's capacity for subdirectories is vast compared to a filing cabinet's capacity for drawers and folders.

In addition to creating directory structures, DOS commands prepare new disks for storing data and verify the reliability of existing disks (Table 1.2).

Table 1.2	*Manual System*	*Electronic System*
Directory and Disk Management: Comparison	Label folders and drawers in a filing cabinet for holding related information	Use DOS to create subdirectories for holding related disk files
	Prepare a new filing cabinet	Use DOS to format a new disk
	Make sure that none of the filing cabinet drawers stick and that all file folders are accessible	Use DOS to check the integrity of a disk and to verify the readability of disk files

FILE- AND DISK-NAMING CONVENTIONS

Before you can perform file and disk management operations, you must first learn the DOS rules for naming files and disk drives.

FILE-NAMING CONVENTIONS

DOS has several rules or conventions for naming files. Although these conventions provide a standard among computer users, they also impose some limitations. For example, a file name of eight characters is hardly sufficient to describe the contents of a file. Nevertheless, you must adhere to the following file-naming conventions to store a file on a disk:

1. A complete file name consists of a file name and an extension, separated by a period (for example, FILENAME.EXT). Every disk file must have a name; however, the extension is often optional. The name of a file reflects its content, while the extension commonly indicates the application software program used to create the file. For example, Microsoft Excel attaches an extension of XLS to its electronic worksheet files and dBase attaches DBF to its database files.

2. A file name can contain one to eight characters, with no spaces.

3. An **extension** can contain one to three characters, with no spaces.

4. Although you can use some special symbols in a file name, such as the ampersand (&) or underscore (_), try to use only letters and numbers. You must avoid symbols that DOS reserves (for example, *, ?, |, <, >).

Refer to Table 1.3 for examples of valid and invalid file names.

Table 1.3	*File Name*	*Status And Reason*
Valid and Invalid File Names	QUARTER	Valid; contains seven characters in the file name and has no extension
	QUARTER1.93	Valid; contains eight characters in the file name and two characters in the extension, separated by a period
	SAMPLEBUD	Invalid; contains more than eight characters in the file name
	A.1993	Invalid; contains more than three characters in the extension (*Note*: Although invalid, this file would still be saved as A.199 with the 3 being truncated from the complete file name.)
	A	Valid; contains one character in the file name and no extension

File name extensions allow you to categorize your work. Some application software programs automatically attach an extension to a file when it is saved to the disk—you simply type the file name. By looking at extensions, you can immediately tell what data files were created by which programs. Other applications, such as some word processing programs, allow you to add your own extension when saving a file.

When creating extensions for file names, you should not use certain letter combinations reserved by DOS and application software programs. Used incorrectly, these extensions can produce conflicts among programs. Table 1.4 provides a summary of common extensions to avoid when naming files.

Table 1.4	Extension	Application	Description
Reserved Extensions	COM	DOS	Command file
	EXE	DOS	Executable file
	SYS	DOS	System file
	BAT	DOS	Batch file
	INI	Windows	Initialization file
	DLL	Windows	Program file
	BAS	Basic	Program file

DISK-DRIVE-NAMING CONVENTIONS

There are several possible disk drive configurations for microcomputers, and knowing how to reference each storage area is crucial to working with DOS. The first diskette drive is always referred to as drive A:. If your computer has two diskette drives, drive A: is usually positioned to the left or above the second diskette drive, called drive B:. If your computer has a hard disk drive, it is referred to as drive C:. The drive letter is always followed by a colon (:) to represent a drive designation.

The computer that you are using may have either two diskette drives (drive A: and drive B:), one diskette drive and a hard disk (drive A: and drive C:), or two diskette drives and a hard disk (drive A:, drive B:, and drive C:). If a computer has more than one hard disk, the additional disks are labeled alphabetically (for example, drive D:, drive E:, and so on).

To refer to a file on a particular disk, preface the file name with the disk drive designation. For example, you would enter a file name of A:BUDGET to save a document called BUDGET onto a diskette in drive A:. Typing C:BUDGET would instruct DOS to save the file on the hard disk drive C:. Notice that there is never a space between the drive designation and the file name.

WORKING WITH DOS

From its introduction in 1981 to the release of DOS 6.2 in 1993, DOS has established itself as the primary operating system for microcomputers. In the same way that application programs are continually updated with new features, the DOS operating system software has been greatly improved over the past few years. One of the primary differences between the initial versions of DOS and the later releases is the inclusion of the DOS Shell. Whereas earlier versions of DOS supplied only the DOS system prompt for entering commands, the DOS Shell enables you to perform file and disk management using a menu system in a graphical environment.

THE COMMAND LINE

Most experienced computer users associate DOS with the command line or DOS system prompt. Although some novice users break out in a cold sweat at the sight of a C:\> prompt on the computer screen, there are many people who prefer the ease of typing commands directly. The advantages of working from the DOS command line include the ability to perform numerous unrelated tasks quickly and freely, without the need to traverse several menus to execute a single command. On the other hand, the command line requires a greater understanding of DOS than that needed for using the DOS Shell.

THE DOS SHELL

The **DOS Shell** is a software program that uses a **graphical user interface** (GUI) for performing DOS commands. A graphical interface makes using computers easier and more intuitive. In the DOS Shell, you use the keyboard or a pointing device called a mouse to select from icons (pictures that represent disks, program files, and data files) rather than typing lengthy commands. Although the DOS Shell employs a standard menu system to access commands, some people find the interface restrictive when compared to the flexibility of the command line.

Because some computers may not have the necessary program files installed for using the DOS Shell, this guide separates its discussions on performing commands using the command line and the DOS Shell. (*Note*: The retail version of DOS 6.2 does not include the DOS Shell program files. You may, however, use the DOS Shell program files from DOS 5.0 or DOS 6.0. To acquire the DOS Shell program files for version 6.2, you must fill out the coupon for the "supplemental disk" provided in the MS-DOS User's Guide and mail it to Microsoft.)

INTERNAL AND EXTERNAL COMMANDS

You instruct DOS to perform a task by typing a command at the system prompt or choosing a command from the DOS Shell menu. How DOS proceeds with your request depends on whether the instruction is an **internal command** or an **external command**. These commands differ in where they are stored when the computer is running.

Internal DOS commands are copied into the computer's RAM (random access memory) from a special file on the disk when you first turn on the computer. Since the computer accesses RAM many times faster than it accesses the disk, DOS places the most frequently used commands in memory. When you turn off the computer, the contents of RAM are discarded.

External DOS commands are stored in program files on the disk. Because these commands are not used as frequently as internal commands, they are not kept in RAM. When you execute an external command, DOS copies the instructions from the program file on the disk to memory, performs the instructions, and then removes the program from memory.

LOADING DOS: THE BOOT PROCESS

DOS is loaded into the computer's RAM when you first turn on the computer. This process is often referred to as *booting* the computer. You perform a **cold boot** when you turn on the computer's power to load DOS. A **warm boot** refers to the process of reloading DOS into RAM when the computer is already turned on. You perform a warm boot when a software program locks or freezes the computer, causing the keyboard to stop responding to your touch. Be forewarned that to reload DOS a warm boot first discards the contents of RAM, so you lose whatever work you have done since you last saved your work to the disk. To warm boot a computer, you press and hold down the [Ctrl]+[Alt] keys simultaneously, tap the [Delete] key, and then release all the keys.

The computer performs the following steps during the boot process:

1. *Checks the equipment.*
   The computer performs a diagnostic check to make sure the hardware peripherals (keyboard, monitor, and so on) are connected properly and RAM is functional. On most computers, a number appears at the top left-hand corner of the screen that represents RAM being checked. This diagnostic process is sometimes referred to as the POST (Power-On Self Test).

2. *Searches for DOS.*
   After completing the POST, the computer looks for DOS in drive A:. If it finds a diskette with DOS, the operating system files are copied from the diskette to RAM. If the computer finds a non-DOS disk in drive A:, an error message appears on the screen informing you that the required DOS files were not found. If no diskette is found in drive A:, the computer proceeds to the hard disk to look for DOS. On most hard disk systems, the computer finds DOS on drive C:.

3. *Loads the DOS operating system files.*
   The computer loads the operating system files into RAM, specifically COMMAND.COM, IO.SYS, and MSDOS.SYS. Although these files are stored together on a disk, the IO.SYS and MSDOS.SYS files are hidden from view to avoid accidental deletion. The IO.SYS file holds the instructions for the basic input and output operations, while the MSDOS.SYS file holds information related to file and disk management. The command processor, COMMAND.COM, contains the internal DOS commands.

4. *Executes commands in the CONFIG.SYS and AUTOEXEC.BAT files.*
   With DOS loaded into RAM, the computer completes the boot process by executing instructions that it finds in the CONFIG.SYS and AUTOEXEC.BAT files. These two files are created by the user and must be stored in the root directory of a disk. The CONFIG.SYS file contains system configuration commands and the AUTOEXEC.BAT file stores commands that you want automatically executed each time the computer is booted. In many cases, the AUTOEXEC.BAT file presents a menu or the DOS Shell to complete the boot process.

DOS 6 can be loaded from the hard disk (drive C:) or from a series of setup diskettes in drive A:. Because DOS 6 consists of a relatively large number of programs, this guide assumes that you are working on a computer with a hard disk. The DOS program files are commonly stored in a subdirectory called \DOS, except for the COMMAND.COM, IO.SYS, and MSDOS.SYS files, which are stored in the root directory.

Perform the following steps to load DOS on your computer.

1. Ensure that there is no diskette in drive A: and that the drive door latch is open (not covering the diskette drive bay). Turn on the power switches to the computer and monitor.

2. As the computer looks for DOS in drive A:, you may see the disk drive light come on and hear a whirring noise. When it cannot find the necessary DOS files, the computer moves its search to drive C:. Depending on the instructions stored in the AUTOEXEC.BAT file, you will be presented with one of the following scenarios:

    a. A prompt to enter a new date usually indicates that the computer did not find an AUTOEXEC.BAT file in the root directory. In this situation, you bypass the date and time prompts and specify where to find the external DOS files. Perform the following commands:
    PRESS: [Enter] twice
    TYPE: path c:\;c:\dos
    PRESS: [Enter]
    TYPE: prompt pg
    PRESS: [Enter]
    The C:\> system prompt should appear on the screen. (*Note*: These commands are usually contained in the AUTOEXEC.BAT file. The PATH and PROMPT commands are covered in Session 3.)

    b. A C:\> prompt indicates that DOS has been successfully loaded.

    c. The words "MS-DOS Shell" appearing at the top of the screen indicate that you have entered the DOS Shell program. To exit the DOS Shell:
    PRESS: [F3] key
    TYPE: cd \
    PRESS: [Enter]
    The C:\> system prompt should appear on the screen. (*Note*: The CD command is covered in Session 3.)

    d. A list of menu choices usually indicates a customized menu system that has been created to provide easy access to the application software programs on your computer. To exit the menu to DOS:
    SELECT: *the appropriate option from the menu*

If you do not see the C:\> system prompt on the screen after making the menu selection, ask your instructor for assistance.

Preparing you for all the possible configurations for loading DOS is impossible. As mentioned previously, the loading process depends on the commands found in the CONFIG.SYS and AUTOEXEC.BAT files. If you experience problems performing any commands in this guide, ask your instructor or lab assistant for help, or refer to the MS-DOS User's Guide.

USING THE KEYBOARD

The keyboard is the primary input device that you use to communicate with the computer. If you are familiar with a typewriter, you will recognize the layout of alphanumeric keys on the keyboard. These keys are used to insert letters, numbers, and punctuation symbols.

There are two special keys labeled (Ctrl) (pronounced Control) and (Alt) (or Alternate) that appear with the alphanumeric keys. The purpose of these two keys is to give every other key on the keyboard an additional meaning. For example, when you press the letter *a* on the keyboard, you give the computer an instruction to place an *a* on the screen. When you press and hold down the (Ctrl) or (Alt) keys and then press *a*, you send a different instruction to the computer. The content or resulting action of the keystroke depends on the software program that you are using.

Function keys are labeled (F1) to (F10) or (F12) and appear above or to the left of the alphanumeric keys. You press a function key to send a special instruction to the computer. Again, how the computer responds to the instruction depends on the software program that you are using. In most application software programs, the (F1) key retrieves help information.

A keyboard that separates the cursor-movement keys from the numeric pad is called an extended or enhanced keyboard. On extended keyboards, the function keys are placed at the top of the keyboard and the cursor-movement keys are positioned between the numeric pad and alphanumeric keys. On standard keyboards, function keys are positioned to the left of the alphanumeric keys. Because standard keyboards combine the cursor-movement keys and the numeric pad, you must press (Num Lock) to toggle between using the keypad to insert numbers or move the cursor.

The (Esc) key, usually located at the top left-hand corner of the keyboard, is used to cancel an activity. If (Esc) is unsuccessful, press (Ctrl) and hold it down while you tap (Break). The (Ctrl)+(Break) key combination tells the computer to halt its current activity and give you control of the system.

To send a copy of the information displayed on the screen to the printer, press (Shift)+(PrtScr). To print what appears on the screen as you enter commands, press (Ctrl)+(PrtScr) to turn on continuous printing. When finished printing, you must turn off continuous printing by pressing (Ctrl)+(PrtScr) a second time. These techniques are useful for printing out the examples and exercises in this guide, but may not work with all brands of printers.

USING THE COMMAND LINE

The majority of experienced computer users prefer to enter DOS commands at the command line. Besides offering greater flexibility and speed, the command line provides a familiar interface for people who have worked with DOS in its earlier releases. This section introduces some special keys on the keyboard and guides you through basic DOS commands using the DOS 6 command line.

ENTERING COMMANDS

Imagine DOS as your new assistant—albeit one with limited intuitiveness. As with any new assistant, you must communicate your instructions and intentions clearly and concisely. DOS expects you to give it unambiguous instructions using correct spelling and **syntax**, similar to using correct grammar when writing or speaking. Also be aware that DOS does not differentiate between commands entered using lower- or uppercase letters.

To instruct DOS to perform a particular task, you type the command and then press (Enter). The (Enter) key tells DOS to execute the command. If you make a mistake when typing, press the (BackSpace) key to remove the mistyped letters and then retype the entry. If you mistype a command and press the (Enter) key, the computer attempts to execute the command and then replies with a "Bad command or file name" message. This message occurs frequently for most people that are first learning DOS.

MOVING FROM DISK TO DISK

One of the first DOS procedures to learn is how to move among the disk storage areas. At the command line, the system prompt contains the letter of the current or **default disk drive**. DOS applies any commands that you enter to the current drive, unless you expressly specify a different drive.

Perform the following steps to move among the disk drives.

1. Ensure that the Advantage Diskette is placed into drive A:. Close the drive door latch, if one is present.

2. To move to drive A:, issue the following command from the C:\> prompt:
    TYPE: a:
    PRESS: [Enter]
    Notice that the system prompt changes to A:\>.

3. Move back to drive C: using the following command:
    TYPE: c:
    PRESS: [Enter]

4. Now try moving to drive Q:. An error message may appear telling you that drive Q is an "Invalid drive specification." (*Note*: On some computers, drive Q: may exist. If your computer displays the Q:\> prompt after entering this command, proceed to the next step.)

5. Move back to drive A:.

SETTING THE CLOCK (DATE AND TIME)

Most computers have a battery-powered internal clock that keeps track of the current date and time, even when the computer is turned off. Using the clock, DOS automatically dates and time stamps all the files that you create in an application. This allows you to easily find the most recent version of a file by comparing the attached dates and times. If your computer does not have an internal clock, you can manually set the current date and time using the following commands:

DATE [*mm-dd-yy*]

TIME [*hh:mm*]

Perform the following steps.

1. Make sure that the A:\> system prompt is displayed.

2. To set the date for the system clock:
   TYPE: date
   PRESS: (Enter)
   The date appears as stored by the system clock.

3. Change the date to September 24, 1994. Type the new date in the format mm-dd-yy (month-day-year):
   TYPE: 9-24-94
   PRESS: (Enter)
   The A:\> system prompt reappears.

4. To change the date to December 31, 1994:
   TYPE: date 12-31-94
   PRESS: (Enter)
   Notice that DOS does not always provide feedback on the success or failure of a command.

5. To change the date to the current date:
   TYPE: date *current date*
   PRESS: (Enter)

6. To set the time for the internal clock:
   TYPE: time
   PRESS: (Enter)
   The time appears as stored by the system clock.

7. Type the new time in 24-hour military format or place a "p" after the time to indicate "pm." For example, if the time is 1:20 P.M., you can type 13:20 or 1:20p. Let's change the time to 2:30 P.M.:
   TYPE: 2:30p
   PRESS: (Enter)
   The A:\> system prompt reappears.

8. To change the system clock to the current time:
   TYPE: time *current time*
   PRESS: (Enter)

Quick Reference   Command: DATE (internal)
DATE and TIME   Syntax: date [*mm-dd-yy*]
Commands   Purpose: Sets the date for the system clock

                          Command: TIME (internal)
                          Syntax: time [*hh:mm*]
                          Purpose: Sets the time for the system clock

DISPLAYING THE DOS VERSION (VER)

The production of software, whether an operating system or an application
program, is an ongoing effort. As hardware continues to improve, software
programs, such as DOS, are rewritten to take advantage of the new
technology. Because of these rapid changes, there are currently several
different versions of DOS being used on microcomputers.

To display the DOS version that exists on your computer, enter the
following command:

>   TYPE: ver
>   PRESS: (Enter)

Quick Reference   Command: VER (internal)
VER Command   Syntax: ver
                          Purpose: Displays the DOS version number

DISPLAYING A LIST OF FILES (DIR)

The most commonly used command in DOS is DIR (an abbreviation for
DIRECTORY). The DIR command provides the table of contents for a
disk by listing the files and subdirectories it contains. A typical line in a
DIR file listing appears as follows:

```
COMMAND     COM        54,619    09-30-93   6:20a
```

The first column of information contains the file name (COMMAND), the
second column provides the extension (COM), the third column specifies
the size of the file in bytes (54,619), and the last two columns provide the

date (09-30-93) and time (6:20a) that the file was last modified. There is also another type of line item that may appear in a directory listing, as shown in this next example:

```
DOS             <DIR>           12-11-93   4:50p
```

The <DIR> is not an extension but rather a subdirectory. A subdirectory is a special type of DOS file that acts like a folder for storing program and data files. Notice that there is no file size associated with a subdirectory.

The basic syntax for the DIR command follows:

DIR [*drive:*] [/P] [/W]

As shown by the square brackets in this syntax diagram, the drive letter, /P switch, and /W switch are optional parameters of the DIR command. The /P switch in the DIR command tells DOS to pause after displaying one screenful of information. Adding the /W switch to the end of a DIR command, tells DOS to display the files across the width of the screen. Perform the following steps to list the files stored on the Advantage Diskette.

1. Make sure that the A:\> system prompt is displayed.

2. List the files on drive A:.
    TYPE: dir
    PRESS: (Enter)
    At the end of the file listing, there are two lines that provide information on how many files are included in the list, their cumulative size, and the amount of free disk space left on drive A:. Your screen should appear similar to Figure 1.1.

Figure 1.1

Displaying files
with the DIR
command.

```
SOFTWARE 4            3,337 09-01-92    4:46p
WPBLOCK  4            8,991 09-01-92    3:59p
HARDWARE ASC         1,440 10-29-92    8:30a
CLIENTS  DBF         2,290 11-09-92   10:48a
EXPENSES DBF         8,994 11-09-92   10:53a
SEMINAR  LET           997 09-17-92    6:52a
SALES    MAR           779 08-31-92    2:29p
EXAMPLE  TXT           500 10-26-92   11:01a
HARDWARE TXT         1,440 10-29-92    8:30a
BILLS    WK1         1,939 08-08-91   12:00p
BUDGET   WK1         2,771 08-08-91   12:00p
EMPLOYEE WK1         2,807 08-11-92    2:28p
INCOME   WK1         3,718 08-08-91   12:00p
Q1       WK1         2,258 08-08-91   12:00p
Q2       WK1         2,258 08-08-91   12:00p
Q3       WK1         2,259 08-08-91   12:00p
Q4       WK1         2,258 08-08-91   12:00p
SALES    WK1         2,655 08-08-91   12:00p
SUMMARY  WK1         2,826 08-08-91   12:00p
CASH     XLS         6,265 08-31-92   12:00p
STATS    XLS         2,246 08-31-92   12:00p
        32 file(s)           104,170 bytes
                             611,328 bytes free

A:\>
```

3. Because the computer screen displays less than 25 rows of information at one time, the information near the top scrolls off the screen to provide room for more file names at the bottom. To display a directory listing one page at a time, add /P to the end of the command:
    TYPE: dir /p
    PRESS: (Enter)
    (*Hint*: Remember that DOS does not distinguish between lower- and uppercase letters when you enter commands.)

4. After filling one screen with information, the listing stops and a message displays at the bottom of the screen asking you to press a key to continue:
    PRESS: Space Bar
    (*Note*: Whenever prompted to "Press a key to continue," you press the Space Bar or the (Enter) key.)

5. To list files across the width of the screen, you use the /W switch:
    TYPE: dir /w
    PRESS: (Enter)
    Notice that some information is not displayed when you use this switch, such as the size of each file and the last modification date and time.

6. To move to drive C:, enter the following command:
    TYPE: c:
    PRESS: (Enter)

7. TYPE: `dir`
   PRESS: [Enter]
   The directory listing shows the files on your hard disk.

8. Although DOS assumes that a command applies to the current disk drive, you can force DOS to display the files in drive A: from the drive C: prompt (C:\>). Perform the following:
   TYPE: `dir a:`
   PRESS: [Enter]
   It is important to enter a space between the DOS command (DIR) and the drive designation (A:).

....

Quick Reference	Command:	DIR (internal)
DIR Command	Syntax:	dir [*drive:*] [/p] [/w]
	Purpose:	Lists the files stored on a disk or in a directory

....

CLEARING THE SCREEN (CLS)

After issuing several DOS commands, the screen may become cluttered with information. The CLS (CLEAR SCREEN) command quickly erases the screen and moves the prompt to the upper left-hand corner.

Enter the following command to clear the screen:

TYPE: `cls`
PRESS: [Enter]

....

Quick Reference	Command:	CLS (internal)
CLS Command	Syntax:	cls
	Purpose:	Clears the screen

....

GETTING HELP (HELP)

Before DOS 5, getting help for DOS meant looking up commands in the reference manual. In DOS 6, there are two methods for retrieving onscreen help for a command: the MS-DOS Help facility and Command Line Help. Both of these methods provide a description of the command and a syntax diagram with the available parameters and switches. A **parameter** is an optional or required variable in a command, such as a file name or disk drive. A **switch** is a modifier that enhances the basic operation of the command. Switches begin with a slash (/) and are followed by a number or letter, like the /P and /W switches for the DIR command.

For example, the syntax diagram for the DEL (DELETE) command shows optional and required parameters, and one switch:

DEL [*drive:*][*path*]*file name* [/P]

Items surrounded by square brackets in a syntax diagram are optional, similar to the layout in the Quick Reference sections in this guide. In this diagram, the drive, path (directory), and /P switch are optional, while the file name parameter is required. In other words, you must include the file name specification when entering this command. The DEL command is used here as an illustration only and will be covered in later sessions.

Perform the following steps.

1. Make sure that the C:\> system prompt is displayed.

2. To access the MS-DOS Help facility, you enter HELP followed by the desired command. For example, do the following:
    TYPE: help dir
    PRESS: (Enter)
    (*Note*: If you receive an error message like "Bad command or file name," DOS cannot find the program files for the MS-DOS HELP facility. To correct this problem, ask your instructor or lab assistant to set a search path to the DOS directory.)

3. To scroll through the Help screen:
    PRESS: (PgDn) repeatedly

4. To move to the top of the DIR Help screen:
    PRESS: (Ctrl)+(Home)

5. To display the table of contents for the MS-DOS Help facility:
    PRESS: (Alt)+c
    (*Note*: If you have a mouse, you can click the mouse pointer on the <Alt+C=Contents> button in the Status bar at the bottom of the Help screen.) Your screen should now appear similar to Figure 1.2.

Figure 1.2

The MS-DOS
Help facility.

Menu
Bar

Status
Bar

Scroll
Bar

```
 File  Search                                                          Help
                        MS-DOS Help: Command Reference
 Use the scroll bars to see more commands. Or, press the PAGE DOWN key. For
 more information about using MS-DOS Help, choose How to Use MS-DOS Help
 from the Help menu, or press F1. To exit MS-DOS Help, press ALT, F, X.

 <What's New in MS-DOS 6.2?>

 <ANSI.SYS>             <Erase>               <Nlsfunc>
 <Append>               <Exit>                <Numlock>
 <Attrib>               <Expand>              <Path>
 <Batch commands>       <Fasthelp>            <Pause>
 <Break>                <Fastopen>            <Power>
 <Buffers>              <Fc>                  <POWER.EXE>
 <Call>                 <Fcbs>                <Print>
 <Cd>                   <Fdisk>               <Prompt>
 <Chcp>                 <Files>               <Qbasic>
 <Chdir>                <Find>                <RAMDRIVE.SYS>
 <Chkdsk>               <For>                 <Rd>
 <CHKSTATE.SYS>         <Format>              <Rem>
 <Choice>               <Goto>                <Ren>
 <Cls>                  <Graphics>            <Rename>
 <Command>              <Help>                <Replace>
 <Alt+C=Contents> <Alt+N=Next> <Alt+B=Back>              00006:00Z
```

6. To return to the Help screen for the DIR command:
   PRESS: Alt+b
   (*Note*: If you have a mouse, you can click the mouse pointer on the
   <Alt+B=Back> button at the bottom of the Help screen.)

7. The MS-DOS Help facility provides *jump terms* that let you move
   quickly to related topics. Using the keyboard, you select jump terms
   using Tab and Shift+Tab. To move through the jump terms
   available in the DIR Help screen, do the following:
   PRESS: Tab repeatedly

8. To view notes on the DIR command:
   SELECT: Notes
   PRESS: Enter
   This instruction tells you to press Tab until the cursor appears on the
   Notes jump term and then press Enter.

9. To move back to the previous Help screen:
   PRESS: Alt+b

10. In this step, you exit the MS-DOS Help facility. To display the File pull-down menu and choose the Exit command:
PRESS: (Alt)+f
TYPE: x
You are returned to the DOS system prompt.

11. To access Command Line Help, you enter the desired command followed by a "/?". For example, do the following:
TYPE: dir /?
PRESS: (Enter)
Your screen should appear similar to Figure 1.3.

Figure 1.3

The Command Line Help facility for the DIR command.

```
Displays a list of files and subdirectories in a directory.

DIR [drive:][path][filename] [/P] [/W] [/A[[:]attribs]] [/O[[:]sortord]]
    [/S] [/B] [/L] [/C[H]]

  [drive:][path][filename]   Specifies drive, directory, and/or files to list.
  /P        Pauses after each screenful of information.
  /W        Uses wide list format.
  /A        Displays files with specified attributes.
  attribs   D  Directories    R  Read-only files      H  Hidden files
            S  System files   A  Files ready to archive  -  Prefix meaning "not"
  /O        List by files in sorted order.
  sortord   N  By name (alphabetic)    S  By size (smallest first)
            E  By extension (alphabetic) D  By date & time (earliest first)
            G  Group directories first   -  Prefix to reverse order
            C  By compression ratio (smallest first)
  /S        Displays files in specified directory and all subdirectories.
  /B        Uses bare format (no heading information or summary).
  /L        Uses lowercase.
  /C[H]     Displays file compression ratio; /CH uses host allocation unit size.

Switches may be preset in the DIRCMD environment variable.  Override
preset switches by prefixing any switch with - (hyphen)--for example, /-W.

C:\>
```

12. Clear the screen.

Quick Reference
HELP Command
Command: HELP (external)
Syntax: help *command* (or *command* /?)
Purpose: Provides help for a DOS command

WORKING WITH THE DOS SHELL

The DOS Shell is a graphical program. To fully appreciate its benefits, you should familiarize yourself with certain mouse actions. Instructions in this guide generally list both the mouse and the keyboard methods for performing commands and procedures. You can try the instructions for each method and decide for yourself which you prefer. This section provides some basic information on how the mouse and the keyboard are used in the DOS Shell.

HOW THE MOUSE IS USED

The mouse is an essential tool for working in a graphical environment. Although it is possible to use the DOS Shell with only a keyboard, much of the program's basic design revolves around the availability of a mouse. Although your mouse may have two or three buttons, the DOS Shell uses only the left mouse button for selecting items and commands.

The primary mouse actions used in the DOS Shell are click, double-click, and drag:

- Click   Press down and release the left mouse button quickly. Clicking is used to select a file, directory, or drive and to choose options from the menu or a dialog box.

- Double-Click   Press down and release the left mouse button twice in rapid succession. Double-clicking is often used to select and execute an action or program.

- Drag   Press down and hold the left mouse button as you move the mouse pointer across the screen. When the mouse pointer reaches the desired location, release the mouse button. Dragging is used to copy and move files.

HOW THE KEYBOARD IS USED

The DOS Shell assigns commonly used commands to function keys. On your keyboard, the function keys may be located to the left or above the alphanumeric typewriter keys. The DOS Shell function key commands are summarized in Table 1.5.

Table 1.5	Key	Alone	Used with Shift	Used with Alt	Used with Ctrl
Function Keys	F1	Help			
	F2				
	F3	Exit DOS Shell			
	F4			Exit DOS Shell	
	F5	Refresh	Repaint Screen		Refresh Area Lists
	F6				
	F7	Move			
	F8	Copy	Add Mode		
	F9	View File Contents	Command Prompt		
	F10	Access Menu Bar			

USING THE DOS SHELL

First introduced in DOS 4, the DOS Shell makes file and disk management easier and provides three important features: drag and drop, task swapping, and file association. The **drag and drop** feature lets you copy and move files by dragging them using a mouse. **Task swapping** allows you to load more than one application program at a time and to switch among them quickly. However, the DOS Shell is not a true **multitasking** environment like Windows or OS/2. **File association** enables you to select a data file and have DOS automatically load the application that was used to create the file. The next few sections describe the parts of the DOS Shell and show you how to access the DOS Shell Help facility.

To load the DOS Shell, perform the following steps.

1. Ensure that the C:\> system prompt is displayed.

2. TYPE: dosshell
   PRESS: [Enter]
   After a few seconds, the DOS Shell appears on the screen (Figure 1.4). If your computer returns an error message, such as "Bad command or file name," ask your instructor or the lab assistant to help locate the DOS Shell program. (*Note*: Your screen may not look exactly like Figure 1.4. The folders and files represent the programs and data that are stored on your hard disk.)

Figure 1.4

The DOS Shell.

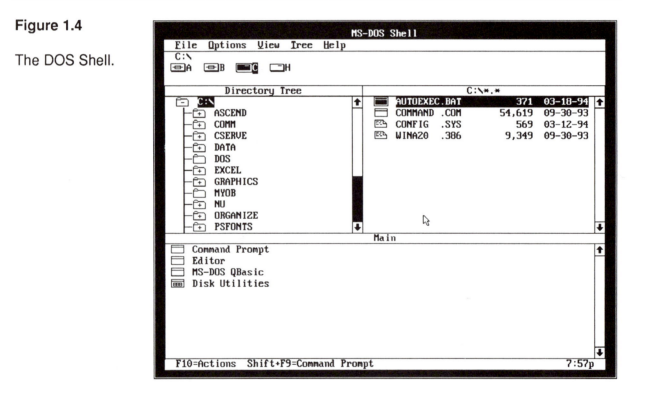

THE GUIDED TOUR

When first loaded, the DOS Shell is divided into the following parts:

Directory Tree area   provides a graphical depiction of the directory structure on the default disk drive

File List area shows the names of the program and data files stored in the highlighted branch of the Directory Tree

Program List area displays a menu of the programs that are accessible from the DOS Shell

A fourth area called the **Active Task List area** is visible only when you enable task swapping. This Active Task List area splits the Program List area in half and shows the names of the open application programs. Figure 1.5 shows all four areas in the DOS Shell.

Other important components of the DOS Shell screen include the Title bar, Menu bar, Current Directory Path, Drive icons, scroll bars, Status bar, and Selection cursor.

Figure 1.5

Parts of the DOS Shell.

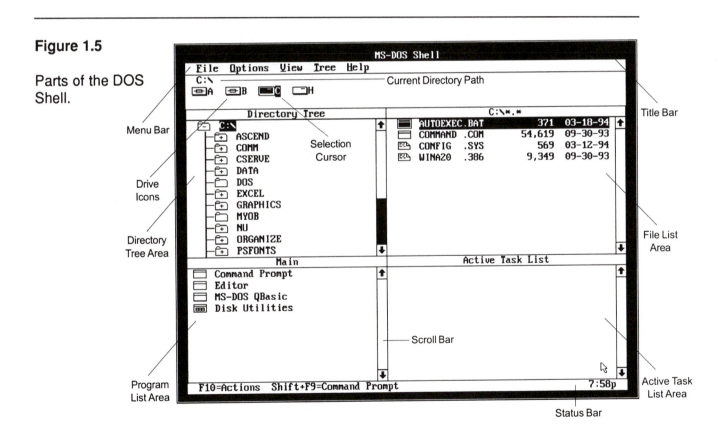

The **Title bar,** located at the top of the screen, contains the name of the application (MS-DOS Shell) or area. In Figure 1.5, the area Title bars display the words Directory Tree (Directory Tree area), C:*.* (File List

area), Main (Program List area), and Active Task List. The Title bar for the active area (containing the Selection cursor) appears in a different color or shade from the other title bars.

The **Menu bar** appears on the second line from the top and contains the commands for copying, renaming, and deleting files, and for customizing the DOS Shell. The Menu bar is accessed by pressing the (Alt) key or the (F10) key.

Appearing immediately below the Menu bar, the **Current Directory Path** displays the full name of the highlighted directory in the Directory Tree area. The **Drive icons**, located below the Path name, represent the available disk drives on your computer. The Directory Tree area displays the directory structure for the highlighted Drive icon.

Scroll bars are placed at the right border of each area in the DOS Shell. The scroll bars facilitate using a mouse to move up and down a list of items in each area. To move one line at a time, you click the up or down arrows at either end of the scroll bar. By dragging the scroll box along the scroll bar, you can move through the list in large steps. The scroll box only appears on a scroll bar when a list of items extends beyond the display portion of the active area.

The **Status bar** is located at the bottom of the screen and displays command options, helpful messages, and the current time.

The **Selection cursor,** or highlighted bar, is used to select a directory in the Directory Tree area, choose files from the File List area, and execute programs from the Program List area.

MOVING THE SELECTION CURSOR

You move the Selection cursor among the different areas in the DOS Shell using the (Tab) key and (Shift)+(Tab) combination. The (Tab) key moves the Selection cursor clockwise, while (Shift)+(Tab) moves the Selection cursor counterclockwise. With a mouse, you simply click in the desired area to move the Selection cursor.

Perform the following steps.

1. PRESS: (Tab)
    You should notice that the area Title bar for the Directory Tree changes color to indicate that it is now active.

2. To move to the File List area:
PRESS: [Tab]

3. To move to the Directory Tree area:
CLICK: Directory Tree Title bar
More specifically, position the mouse pointer over the Directory Tree Title bar and then click the left mouse button once to move the Selection cursor.

4. In the Directory Tree area, move the Selection cursor to the DOS subdirectory or folder:
PRESS: [↓] until DOS is highlighted
Note: Your subdirectory for DOS may be named something different than DOS, such as DOS6 or MSDOS6. Your screen should now appear similar to Figure 1.6.

Figure 1.6

Selecting the DOS directory in the Directory Tree area.

```
                              MS-DOS Shell
  File  Options  View  Tree  Help
  C:\DOS
  ⊟A   ⊟B   ⊟C   ⊟H

         Directory Tree                    C:\DOS\*.*
  ⊟  C:\                        ↑    4201    .CPI     6,404   06-16-92  ↑
    ┌⊞  ASCEND                      4208    .CPI       720   06-16-92
    ├⊞  COMM                        5202    .CPI       395   06-16-92
    ├⊞  CSERVE                      ANSI    .SYS     9,065   09-30-93
    ├⊞  DATA                        APPEND  .EXE    10,774   09-30-93
    ├⊟  DOS                         APPNOTES.TXT     8,723   06-16-92
    ├⊞  EXCEL                       ASSIGN  .COM     6,399   06-16-92
    ├⊞  GRAPHICS                    ATTRIB  .EXE    11,208   09-30-93
    ├⊟  MYOB                        AUTOEXEC.BAT       292   03-01-94
    ├⊞  NU                          AUTOEXEC.UMB       292   03-12-94
    ├⊞  ORGANIZE                    CHKDSK  .EXE    12,241   09-30-93
    ├⊞  PSFONTS                ↓    CHKLIST .MS      3,024   03-07-94  ↓
                                         Main
  ⊟  Command Prompt                                                   ↑
  ⊟  Editor
  ⊟  MS-DOS QBasic
  ⊞  Disk Utilities



                                                                     ↓
  F10=Actions   Shift+F9=Command Prompt                        8:10p
```

5. To move to the File List area:
PRESS: [Tab]

6. Use the cursor-movement keys to scroll through the list of file names:
    PRESS: ⬇ repeatedly
    PRESS: ⬆ repeatedly

7. Use the mouse to scroll down the list of items in the File List area:
    CLICK: down arrow, located at the bottom of the scroll bar
    Each click of the down arrow represents one press of the ⬇ key.

8. To use the mouse to scroll to the top of the file names, first position the mouse pointer over the scroll box on the File List scroll bar.

9. CLICK: left mouse button and hold it down
    DRAG: the scroll box to the top of the scroll bar

10. Release the mouse button.

Quick Reference
Moving Around the DOS Shell

- PRESS: Tab to move clockwise
- PRESS: Shift + Tab to move counterclockwise
- CLICK: the desired area with a mouse
- Use the cursor-movement keys or the scroll bar to move through the items in the active area.

MENU BAR

Commands are grouped together on the Menu bar. To execute a command, you select the appropriate option from the Menu bar and then choose the desired command from the pull-down menu. Commands on the pull-down menu that are not available for selection appear dimmed. Commands that require further information to be collected in a dialog box before executing are followed by an ellipsis (...).

To execute a command using the mouse, click once on the Menu bar option to display the pull-down menu and then click once on the command you want to execute. To execute a command using the keyboard, hold down the Alt key and then tap the underlined or highlighted letter of the desired option on the Menu bar. When the pull-down menu is displayed, press the underlined or highlighted letter of the command you want to execute. Another method for accessing the Menu bar is to press the F10 key and then move through the menus using the cursor-movement keys. To execute a command, highlight the command and press Enter.

You will often see commands appearing in this guide written in the form Help, Index, where Help is the Menu bar option and Index is the command to be selected from the pull-down menu. To practice navigating through the Menu bar, perform the following steps.

1. To access the menu using a mouse:
    CHOOSE: Options from the Menu bar
    Move the mouse pointer over the word Options in the Menu bar and click the left mouse button once. A pull-down menu appears with a list of commands from which to choose. Notice the commands that are followed by an ellipsis (...).

2. To turn on the Task Swapper and display the Active Task List area:
    CHOOSE: Enable Task Swapper
    Move the mouse pointer over the command and click the left mouse button once. Notice that the Program List area is divided in half with the Program List on the left and the Active Task List on the right.

3. To turn off the Task Swapper and remove the Active Task List area, let's choose the Options command using the keyboard:
    PRESS: Alt+o
    This instruction tells you to press and hold down the Alt key and then to tap the letter o. Once enacted, the Options pull-down menu appears.

4. Notice that the Enable Task Swapper command has a bullet beside the command, indicating that the option is active. To turn this feature off:
    TYPE: e
    As shown in this step, you can choose a command from the Menu bar or a pull-down menu by pressing its underlined or highlighted letter.

DIALOG BOXES

The DOS Shell uses dialog boxes (Figure 1.7) to collect information necessary to execute a command. An ellipsis (...) following a command on a pull-down menu means a dialog box appears when the command is selected. Dialog boxes are also used to display messages or ask for confirmation of commands.

Figure 1.7

A dialog box.

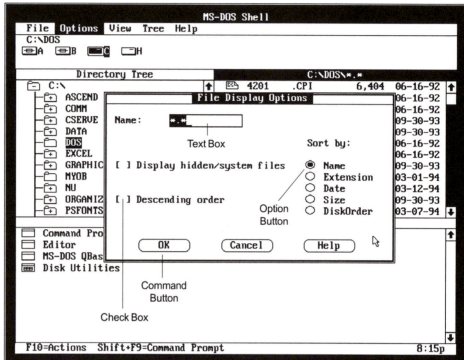

A dialog box uses several methods for collecting information, including list boxes, text boxes, check boxes, option buttons, and command buttons. You can access an item in the dialog box by using the mouse or by pressing the [Tab] key to move clockwise and [Shift]+[Tab] to move counterclockwise around the dialog box.

Study Table 1.6 for information on the various elements of dialog boxes.

Table 1.6

Parts of a Dialog Box

Element	Description
List box	A scrollable list of choices
Text box	A box for collecting typed information
Check box	An option that can be turned on or off
Option button	One option selected from a group of related options
Command button	A button that executes an action when selected

GETTING HELP

The DOS Shell provides context-sensitive help. In other words, you press the (F1) key when you need to retrieve Help information for your current position in the program. You can also use the Help option on the Menu bar for accessing specific Help topics (Table 1.7).

	Command	Description
Table 1.7	*Command*	*Description*
The Help Menu	Index	A general subject and topical index
	Keyboard	Keyboard shortcuts and other tips
	Shell Basics	Information on using the DOS Shell
	Commands	Description of the menu commands
	Procedures	"How to..." section for specific procedures
	Using Help	Information on using the DOS Shell Help facility
	About Shell	Version number and copyright notification

Once a Help window is displayed, the DOS Shell provides several command buttons at the bottom of the window: Close, Back, Keys, Index, and Help. The Close button closes a Help window, similarly to pressing (Esc). The Back button returns to the previous Help window or topic. The remaining choices mirror their menu commands—the Keys button provides keyboard shortcuts, the Index button displays a general subject index, and the Help button shows information on using the DOS Shell Help facility.

Perform the following steps to access the Help facility.

1. CHOOSE: Help, Index
   The MS-DOS Shell Help Index appears, as shown in Figure 1.8.

Figure 1.8

Accessing the
DOS Shell Help
facility.

```
                                    MS-DOS Shell
    File  Options  View  Tree  Help
    C:\DOS
     ▭A   ▭B   ▭C   ▭H                               ⤢
                              MS-DOS Shell Help
    ┌──────────────────────────────────────────────────────────────┐
    │                      MS-DOS Shell Help Index              2 ↑ │
    │  To see a topic:                                      ↑  2    │
    │                                                          2    │
    │   - Double-click the topic.                              3    │
    │                                                          3    │
    │  Or                                                      2    │
    │                                                          2    │
    │   - Press TAB to select the topic you want, and then press ENTER. 3 │
    │                                                          4    │
    │  KEYBOARD HELP                                           4    │
    │  ────────────                                            4    │
    │  ▐General MS-DOS Shell Keys▌                             3    │
    │  ▐Movement Keys▌                                       4 ↓  │
    │                                                        ↓      │
    │                                                               │
    │   ( Close )    ( Back )    ( Keys )    ( Index )   ( Help )   │
    └──────────────────────────────────────────────────────────────┘
                                                                 ↑

                                                                 ↓
    F10=Actions   Shift+F9=Command Prompt                      8:17p
```

2. To browse through the contents of the Help window:
   PRESS: cursor-movement keys (⬆ and ⬇) or click on the arrows at
   the top and bottom of the scroll bar

3. To move through the choices in the index:
   PRESS: Tab several times to move down through the choices, and
   then Shift+Tab to move back up
   (*Note*: When you Tab through the choices, the screen does not
   automatically scroll up. The Selection cursor moves to the command
   buttons once the bottom of the window is reached.)

4. After reading the Help information, close the window:
   PRESS: Esc or CLICK: Close

5. To access context-sensitive help for the Enable Task Swapper
   command in the Menu bar:
   PRESS: Alt+o
   The Options pull-down menu appears.

6. PRESS: ⬇ four times to highlight the Enable Task Swapper
   command. Do not press Enter.

7. PRESS: F1
   A Help window for the Enable Task Swapper command is displayed.

8. After reading the Help information, close the window:
   PRESS: Esc or CLICK: Close

....

Quick Reference   1. PRESS: F1 to display context-sensitive help
Using Help   2. Highlight an option on a pull-down menu and then:
                         PRESS: F1 to display context-sensitive help for a menu command
                      3. PRESS: Esc or CLICK: Close button to close a Help window

....

ACCESSING THE COMMAND LINE

Although you can perform common file and disk management tasks from the DOS Shell, there are some commands that are only available from the command line. To perform these commands, you must permanently or temporarily leave the DOS Shell. This section concentrates on the methods for temporarily leaving the DOS Shell.

Perform the following steps.

1. To temporarily leave the DOS Shell and display the command line:
   PRESS: Shift+F9
   The C:\DOS> system prompt appears. Notice that the prompt reflects the name of the subdirectory that was last highlighted in the Directory Tree area of the DOS Shell.

2. At this point, you can enter a DOS command. For this example, enter the following:
   TYPE: dir /w
   PRESS: Enter

3. To return to the DOS Shell:
   TYPE: exit
   PRESS: Enter
   The DOS Shell immediately reappears.

   CAUTION: Do not return to the DOS Shell from the command line by typing dosshell and pressing Enter. This command would load a second copy of the DOS Shell into memory.

4. To temporarily leave the DOS Shell using the mouse:
    DOUBLE-CLICK: Command Prompt option in the Program List area

5. When the command line appears, return to the DOS Shell.

EXITING THE DOS SHELL

Some application software programs may not work correctly with the DOS Shell loaded in memory, and, therefore, you must exit the DOS Shell permanently and load the program from the command line. You exit the DOS Shell by choosing File, Exit from the Menu bar or by pressing [F3].

Execute the following command to leave the DOS Shell:

CHOOSE: File, Exit

SUMMARY

This session introduced you to the most popular operating system for microcomputers, MS-DOS. An operating system is a collection of software programs that enables you to interact with the computer. Besides controlling the input and output functions, an operating system provides the tools for file and disk management.

There are two methods for using DOS: the command line and the DOS Shell. From the command line, you give DOS instructions by typing in commands and pressing Enter. The DOS Shell, on the other hand, provides a graphical environment and allows you to choose commands from pull-down menus using a mouse or the keyboard. Although the DOS Shell is easier to learn, the command line is often preferred by experienced computer users for its greater flexibility.

Many of the commands and procedures introduced in this session appear in the Command Summary (Table 1.8).

Table 1.8	*Command*	*Description*
Command Summary	DATE	Sets the date for the system clock
	TIME	Sets the time for the system clock
	VER	Displays the DOS version number
	DIR	Lists the files stored on a disk or in a directory
	CLS	Clears the screen
	HELP	Provides help for a DOS command
DOS Shell Commands	Help, Index (F1)	Displays a general subject and topical index
	Command Prompt (Shift+F9)	Temporarily leaves the DOS Shell; to return, type exit at the command line and press Enter
	File, Exit (F3)	Exits the DOS Shell

KEY TERMS

Active Task List area   Area of the DOS Shell that shows the names of open application programs.

cold boot   Starting a computer by turning on the power and loading the operating system into RAM (random access memory).

Current Directory Path   The highlighted subdirectory in the DOS Shell; files in the File List area represent the contents of the Current Directory Path.

data files   Disk files that contain work that was created or entered using DOS or an application software program.

default disk drive   The current disk drive. The disk drive that is automatically affected by commands unless the user specifically names a different drive.

directory structure   See *directory tree*.

directory tree   The organization of subdirectories on a hard disk or floppy diskette. The root directory appears at the top of the directory tree and subdirectories branch out from the root directory.

Directory Tree area   Area of the DOS Shell that provides a graphical depiction of the directory structure on the default disk drive.

DOS Shell   A software program that provides a graphical interface for performing file and disk management tasks.

drag and drop   A feature of the DOS Shell that enables you to copy and move files by dragging them using a mouse.

Drive icons   Located beneath the Path name in the DOS Shell, the Drive icons represent the available disk drives on your computer.

extension   One to three characters added to a file name to aid in file identification. The file name and extension are separated by a period.

external commands   DOS command instructions that are not loaded into RAM when you boot the computer. These commands are part of the operating system and are stored in program files on the disk.

file association   The process of associating a file type (extension) with an application software program. You can start an application and load a file by double-clicking on an associated data file in the DOS Shell.

File List area   Area of the DOS Shell that shows the names of the program and data files stored in the selected or highlighted branch of the Directory Tree.

graphical user interface   Software feature that makes programs easier to use, and typically employs a mouse. Examples are the DOS Shell, OS/2, Microsoft Windows, and the Macintosh.

internal commands   DOS commands that are loaded into RAM when you boot the computer.

Menu bar   Located at the top of the screen in the DOS Shell, the Menu bar enables easy access to commands and procedures.

multitasking   Activity in which more than one task or program is executed at a time.

operating system   A collection of software programs that manage, coordinate, and control the computer hardware, input and output tasks, and storage system.

parameter   A variable, such as a file name or disk drive, that you use when giving the computer a command.

program files   Disk files that contain instructions for the CPU to perform specific tasks or operations.

Program List area   Area of the DOS Shell that displays a menu of the programs and program groups that are accessible from the DOS Shell.

root directory   In the hierarchy of the directory structure, the first or topmost directory is the root directory.

scroll bars   Scroll bars allow you to move or scroll through an area in the DOS Shell using a mouse.

Selection cursor   The highlighted bar in the DOS Shell that you use to select a directory, choose files, and execute programs.

Status bar   Area of the DOS Shell, appearing at the bottom of the screen, that provides information about the available commands and the current time.

subdirectories   In the hierarchy of the directory structure, subdirectories appear beneath the root directory. Subdirectories store related programs and data files.

switch   Enhancement that provides an additional form of a DOS command; switches begin with a forward slash (/).

syntax   Rules for using a command. The syntax of a DOS command is similar to the grammatical rules for a language.

task swapping   A DOS Shell feature that enables you to load more than one program at a time and to move among them freely. Task swapping does not multitask programs, as Windows and OS/2 do; it suspends tasks when they are not being used.

Title bar   The Title bar contains the name of the application or area. The area with the colored or shaded Title bar represents the active area.

warm boot   Reloading DOS into RAM after the computer has been turned on. To perform a warm boot, press and hold down the Ctrl + Alt keys, tap the Delete key, and then release all keys.

EXERCISES

SHORT ANSWER

1. Briefly explain the purpose of an operating system.
2. Provide some examples of file management tasks.
3. Provide some examples of directory and disk management tasks.
4. What is the difference between internal and external DOS commands?
5. What are the components of a file name? Give three examples.
6. What command displays a list of the files on a disk? List two switches that modify how this command displays files, as covered in this session.
7. Specify two methods for retrieving help on the VER command.
8. What is the DOS Shell?
9. List the four major areas of the DOS Shell.
10. How would you temporarily leave the DOS Shell to enter commands from the command line? How would you return to the DOS Shell?

HANDS-ON

(*Note*: In the following exercises, you perform DOS commands using files located on the Advantage Diskette.)

1. The objective of this exercise is to practice some of the DOS commands that you entered from the command line in this session. For this exercise, you require a blank sheet of paper and a pen to write down information that appears on the screen.
   a. Turn on the computer. During the POST (Power-On Self Test), you will see numbers appear in the top left-hand corner of the screen. These numbers represent the RAM check. When finished, the computer begins its search for the operating system. Write down the final number (the total RAM capacity in KB) that appears in the top-left hand corner.
   b. Ensure that you have a C:\> system prompt on your screen. For assistance, refer to the Loading DOS section or ask your instructor.
   c. Place the Advantage Diskette in drive A:.
   d. Move to drive A:.
   e. Perform a directory listing using the DIR command.
   f. Write down the number of files stored on the Advantage Diskette.
   g. Write down the accumulated size of these files in bytes.
   h. Write down the free space that is available on the disk.
   i. Perform a directory listing of drive C: from the A:\> system prompt. In other words, do not move to drive C: first.
   j. Write down the number of files, the accumulated size of these files, and the available free space on drive C:.
   k. Move to drive P:. In most cases, you will get an error message. Write down the error message. (*Note*: Some computers may have a drive P:. If so, move back to drive A: and proceed to the next step.)
   l. Perform a directory listing so that the files fill one screen at a time.
   m. Perform a directory listing so that the files appear across the width of the screen. Your screen should appear similar to Figure 1.9.

Figure 1.9

Using the DIR
command.

```
Q4        WK1       2,258 08-08-91   12:00p
SALES     WK1       2,655 08-08-91   12:00p
SUMMARY   WK1       2,826 08-08-91   12:00p
CASH      XLS       6,265 08-31-92   12:00p
STATS     XLS       2,246 08-31-92   12:00p
         32 file(s)         104,170 bytes
                            611,328 bytes free

A:\>dir /w

 Volume in drive A has no label
 Volume Serial Number is 1049-1ADD
 Directory of A:\

BUDGET          HARDWARE        NAMES         WPMICRO        WPSPELL
WPTEMP          SOFTWARE.1      WPBLOCK.1     WPTEMP.2       WPBLOCK.3
WPSPELL.3       SOFTWARE.4      WPBLOCK.4     HARDWARE.ASC   CLIENTS.DBF
EXPENSES.DBF    SEMINAR.LET     SALES.MAR     EXAMPLE.TXT    HARDWARE.TXT
BILLS.WK1       BUDGET.WK1      EMPLOYEE.WK1  INCOME.WK1     Q1.WK1
Q2.WK1          Q3.WK1          Q4.WK1        SALES.WK1      SUMMARY.WK1
CASH.XLS        STATS.XLS
         32 file(s)         104,170 bytes
                            611,328 bytes free

A:\>
```

    n. Move to drive C:.

    o. Perform a directory listing. Write down the method for differentiating a subdirectory from a file in this directory listing.

    p. Perform a directory listing so that the files appear across the width of the screen. Write down the method for differentiating a subdirectory from a file in this type of directory listing.

2. This exercise continues to practice some of the DOS commands that you entered from the command line in this session.

    a. Ensure that you have a C:\> system prompt on your screen.

    b. Enter a DOS command to display the DOS version number.

    c. Enter a DOS command to clear the screen.

    d. Using the Command Line Help facility, retrieve help for the DATE command. Write down the syntax for the command as it appears on the screen.

    e. Using the MS-DOS Help facility, retrieve help for the TIME command. Write down the syntax for the command.

    f. Perform a directory listing of drive A: from the C:\> system prompt, so that the files are listed across the width of the screen. Write down the command.

    g. Clear the screen.

3. This exercise practices working with the DOS
on moving the Selection cursor and accessing t'
a. Load the DOS Shell from the C:\> system
b. Select the root directory in the Directory Tree .
c. Make the File List area active.
d. Access the Help facility for Commands in the DOS Shell. Your
screen should appear similar to Figure 1.10.

Figure 1.10

Help for
Commands in
the DOS Shell.

e. Request Help for the File, Exit command. Write down the brief
summary appearing at the top of the window.
f. Request Help for the Options, Enable Task Swapper command.
Write down the brief summary appearing at the top of the window.
g. Use the Index command button to display the Help Index.
h. Find the keyboard methods for moving directly to the top and
bottom of a list box. Write down the two key combinations. (*Hint*:
Look for a Help topic on dialog boxes.)
i. Exit the DOS Shell.

DOS 6:
MANAGING YOUR FILES

With only a few simple DOS commands, you can perform all your everyday file management procedures from the command line or the DOS Shell. Whether you need to copy or move a file from the hard disk to a floppy diskette, rename a data file, or delete an entire disk's contents, DOS file management commands enable you to complete your filing duties quickly and easily.

PREVIEW

When you have completed this session, you will be able to:

Use wildcard characters to select groups of files.

•

Copy, move, rename, and delete a file from the command line.

•

Recover an accidentally deleted file.

•

View the contents of a text file from the command line.

•

Change the attributes of a file.

•

Customize the display of the DOS Shell.

•

Select a file or group of files from the DOS Shell.

•

Copy, move, rename, and delete a file from the DOS Shell.

•

View the contents of a file from the DOS Shell.

•

Change the attributes of a file from the DOS Shell.

Why Is This Session Important?
Using the Command Line
       More Options for Listing Files (DIR)
       Selecting Files
       Copying Files (COPY)
       Moving Files (MOVE)
       Renaming Files (REN)
       Deleting Files (DEL)
       Undeleting Files (UNDELETE)
       Viewing the Contents of a File (TYPE)
       Displaying File Attributes (ATTRIB)
Using the DOS Shell
       Customizing the Display
       Selecting Files
       Copying and Moving Files
       Renaming Files
       Deleting Files
       Undeleting Files
       Viewing the Contents of a File
       Changing the File Attributes
Summary
       Command Summary
Key Terms
Exercises
       Short Answer
       Hands-On

WHY IS THIS SESSION IMPORTANT?

This session introduces the procedures for managing files stored on hard disks and floppy diskettes. The file management commands introduced here will help you perform the following functions on your computer:

• Copy data files from your hard disk to a floppy diskette, so you can access them using a different computer.

• Change the names of documents to make them more indicative of their contents. For example, you may want to change a file's name from BUDGET.WK3 to BUDGET94.WK3.

• Remove old program and data files to free up disk space for loading newer software programs.

In this session, you perform these types of tasks from the command line using the following DOS commands:

ATTRIB	DEL	REN
COPY	MOVE	TYPE

Before proceeding, make sure the following are true:

1. You have turned on your computer system.
2. The C:\> system prompt is displayed on the screen.
3. Your Advantage Diskette is inserted into drive A:. You will work with files on the diskette that have been created for you.

USING THE COMMAND LINE

The majority of file management tasks are performed using relatively few DOS commands. This section introduces the COPY, MOVE, REN, and DEL commands for copying, moving, renaming, and deleting files. To conclude the section, you use the TYPE command to display the contents of a text file and the ATTRIB command to change a file's attributes.

MORE OPTIONS FOR LISTING FILES (DIR)

The DIR command provides several switches that modify or enhance its basic operation. You have already used the /P switch to list files one screen at a time and the /W switch to list files across the width of the screen. This section introduces two more DIR switches: the /O switch sorts a directory listing and the /A switch displays files with a particular file attribute. The DIR switches are summarized in Table 2.1.

Table 2.1	Switch	Description	Example
DIR Command Switches	/P	Displays files one page at a time	dir /p
	/W	Displays files across the width of the screen	dir /w
	/O	Displays files in a sorted order using the following sort keys:	
		N — by name	dir /on
		E — by extension	dir /oe
		S — by size	dir /os
		D — by date and time	dir /od
		You precede the sort key with a minus sign to reverse the order.	dir /o-n
	/A	Displays files matching a particular attribute:	
		R — read-only	dir /ar
		A — archive	dir /aa
		S — system	dir /as
		H — hidden	dir /ah
		You precede the attribute with a minus sign to mean "not including." Attributes are discussed later in this session.	dir /a-r

Perform the following steps.

1. Ensure that the Advantage Diskette is placed into drive A: and that the C:\> system prompt is displayed.

2. Move to drive A:.

3. To list the files on drive A:, enter the following command:
    TYPE: `dir`
    PRESS: (Enter)

4. To list the files sorted by their extensions:
    TYPE: `dir /oe`
    PRESS: (Enter)
    You place the sort key (*e* for extension) immediately after the /O switch. There are no spaces between the key and the switch.

5. To list the files by their size, sorted in descending order:
    TYPE: `dir /o-s`
    PRESS: (Enter)
    The minus sign must precede the sort key (*s* for size) to reverse the natural ascending sort order.

6. To list the files, sorted by file name, across the width of the screen:
    TYPE: `dir /on /w`
    PRESS: (Enter)
    Notice that you can use more than one switch at a time with the DIR command. Your screen should appear similar to Figure 2.1.

Figure 2.1

A directory listing sorted by file name across the width of the screen.

```
NAMES             966 09-01-92  10:07a
WPTEMP            905 08-31-92   3:16p
BUDGET            897 08-31-92   3:48p
SALES     MAR     779 08-31-92   2:29p
EXAMPLE   TXT     500 10-26-92  11:01a
         32 file(s)      104,170 bytes
                         611,328 bytes free

A:\>dir /on /w

 Volume in drive A has no label
 Volume Serial Number is 1049-1ADD
 Directory of A:\

BILLS.WK1      BUDGET        BUDGET.WK1    CASH.XLS     CLIENTS.DBF
EMPLOYEE.WK1   EXAMPLE.TXT   EXPENSES.DBF  HARDWARE     HARDWARE.ASC
HARDWARE.TXT   INCOME.WK1    NAMES         Q1.WK1       Q2.WK1
Q3.WK1         Q4.WK1        SALES.MAR     SALES.WK1    SEMINAR.LET
SOFTWARE.1     SOFTWARE.4    STATS.XLS     SUMMARY.WK1  WPBLOCK.1
WPBLOCK.3      WPBLOCK.4     WPMICRO       WPSPELL      WPSPELL.3
WPTEMP         WPTEMP.2
         32 file(s)      104,170 bytes
                         611,328 bytes free

A:\>
```

···

Quick Reference   Command: DIR (internal)
DIR Command   Syntax: dir [*drive:*] [/p] [/w] [/o[-][n,e,s,d]] [/a[-][r,a,s,h]]
Switches   Purpose: Lists the files stored on a disk or in a directory

···

SELECTING FILES

A hard disk can store thousands of files. Consider the amount of time and effort that would be required to manage these files individually. Not a menial task! Fortunately, DOS allows you to apply commands to entire groups of files using a **file specification**. You create a file specification using the DOS **wildcard characters**: the asterisk (*) and the question mark (?). These wildcard symbols are used to represent letters, numbers, or symbols in a file name, similarly to using wild cards in a card game. You use the asterisk (*) to represent a group of characters, a file name, or an extension. You use the question mark (?) to represent a place holder for a single character in a file name.

Table 2.2 provides some examples of using the DOS wildcard characters.

	File Specification	*Description*
Table 2.2		
Wildcard Characters	*.*	Any file name and any extension. For example, BUDGET.DOC, CAR.MEM, and COMMAND.COM. This file specification matches all files.
	*.MEM	Any file name with MEM as the extension. For example, this file specification matches the files CAR.MEM and VACATION.MEM.
	C*.*	The file name begins with the letter *C*, ends with any group of characters, and has any extension. For example, CAR.MEM and COMMAND.COM.
	BUD199?.DOC	File begins with BUD199, ends with a single character in the file name, and has DOC as the extension. For example, BUD1991.DOC, BUD1992.DOC, and BUD1993.DOC.

Perform the following steps to practice using wildcards.

1. Ensure that the A:\> system prompt is displayed.

2. Display a directory listing of all the files on drive A:.
   TYPE: dir *.*
   PRESS: (Enter)
   Most users verbalize the *.* file specification as "star dot star."

3. To limit a directory listing to files that have an extension of WK1:
   TYPE: dir *.wk1
   PRESS: (Enter)
   Only the files that have an extension of WK1 are listed by the DIR command. The * represents any file name in this example.

4. To limit a directory listing to files that begin with the letter *w*:
   TYPE: dir w*.*
   PRESS: (Enter)
   Your screen should appear similar to Figure 2.2.

Figure 2.2

A directory listing of files beginning with the letter *w*.

```
Q3        WK1      2,259 08-08-91  12:00p
Q4        WK1      2,258 08-08-91  12:00p
SALES     WK1      2,655 08-08-91  12:00p
SUMMARY   WK1      2,826 08-08-91  12:00p
        10 file(s)          25,749 bytes
                           611,328 bytes free

A:\>dir w*.*

 Volume in drive A has no label
 Volume Serial Number is 1049-1ADD
 Directory of A:\

WPMICRO          2,870 09-01-92   4:39p
WPSPELL          4,447 08-08-91  12:00p
WPTEMP             905 08-31-92   3:16p
WPBLOCK   1      8,989 08-08-91  12:00p
WPTEMP    2      1,810 08-31-92   3:24p
WPBLOCK   3      8,989 08-08-91  12:00p
WPSPELL   3      2,782 09-01-92  10:07a
WPBLOCK   4      8,991 09-01-92   3:59p
         8 file(s)          39,783 bytes
                           611,328 bytes free

A:\>
```

5. To limit the directory listing to files that have only a single character for their extension:
TYPE: `dir *.?`
PRESS: [Enter]
Note that the question mark represents a place holder for a single character. All files that have either no characters or a maximum of one character for their extension will be included in the directory listing.

6. Clear the screen.

Quick Reference
DOS Wildcards

- Asterisk (*)   Represents a group of characters, a file name, or an extension
- Question Mark (?)   Represents a place holder for a single character in a file specification

---

COPYING FILES (COPY)

Although there are several reasons for copying files, the most important reason is to back up important data. Using the COPY command, you can copy files from one storage location to another or from one file name to another. Most commonly, you use the COPY command to copy files from a hard disk to a floppy diskette. If you work with crucial information on a hard disk, you should keep a diskette copy of the data in a different location to protect it from fire and theft hazards.

CAUTION: It is an infringement on copyright law to make and distribute copies of files from application software programs.

To duplicate files, enter the COPY command using the following syntax:

COPY *source destination*

Perform the following steps from the A:\> system prompt.

1. This example copies a file called EXAMPLE.TXT, stored on the Advantage Diskette, to a file called EXAMPLE.BAK. To perform the copy procedure:
TYPE: `copy example.txt example.bak`
PRESS: [Enter]

Notice that you enter a complete file specification (file name and extension) for the source and destination parameters.

2. To list all files that have EXAMPLE as the file name:
   TYPE: dir example.*
   PRESS: [Enter]
   In the directory listing, you should see the EXAMPLE.TXT file and an EXAMPLE.BAK file.

3. To copy the new file to the hard disk:
   TYPE: copy example.bak c:
   PRESS: [Enter]
   Note that the destination parameter is drive C:. To copy a file to a new storage location and retain the original name, you do not need to enter the file name for the destination.

4. Move to drive C:.

5. To list all files beginning with the letter *e*:
   TYPE: dir e*.*
   PRESS: [Enter]
   The EXAMPLE.BAK file should appear in the listing.

6. To copy all the files with a BAK extension from the hard disk to the Advantage Diskette:
   TYPE: copy *.bak a:

7. If you are using DOS 6.0 or earlier, DOS carries out the COPY command without interruption. However, DOS 6.2 provides a safety feature that warns you when there exists a file on the destination disk with the same name as the source file. In these cases, DOS displays a prompt asking for confirmation before replacing the destination file. Therefore, DOS 6.2 users need to perform the following command before proceeding to step 8:
   TYPE: y (for Yes)
   PRESS: [Enter]

8. Move to drive A:.

9. To list the files in drive A: with an extension of BAK:
   TYPE: dir *.bak
   PRESS: [Enter]

10. Clear the screen.

....

Quick Reference   Command: COPY (internal)
COPY Command   Syntax: copy *source destination*
                       Purpose: Makes a duplicate of one or more files

....

MOVING FILES (MOVE)

When you use the COPY command, the original or source file is left intact
and a new copy of the file is placed in the destination drive or directory. In
previous versions of DOS, you moved a file by first copying it to a new
location and then deleting the original. Introduced in DOS 6, the file
management command MOVE lets you move files quickly.

You enter the MOVE command using the following syntax:

MOVE *source destination*

Perform the following steps from the A:\> system prompt.

1. Ensure that the A:\> system prompt is displayed.

2. To move the file called SEMINAR.LET to drive C:, do the following:
    TYPE: move seminar.let c:
    PRESS: [Enter]

    CAUTION: Because the MOVE command is an external command,
    DOS needs to know where the DOS files are kept on the hard disk. If
    DOS cannot find the MOVE command and an error message appears,
    ask your instructor or lab assistant for help.

3. To see if the file exists on the Advantage Diskette:
    TYPE: dir *.let
    PRESS: [Enter]
    You should see a "File not found" message.

4. To see if the file exists on the hard disk:
    TYPE: dir c:*.let
    PRESS: [Enter]
    The file SEMINAR.LET appears in the directory listing.

Your screen should appear similar to Figure 2.3.

Figure 2.3

Moving a file from
the Advantage
Diskette to the
hard disk drive C:.

```
A:\>move seminar.let c:
a:\seminar.let => c:\seminar.let [ok]

A:\>dir *.let

 Volume in drive A has no label
 Volume Serial Number is 1049-1ADD
 Directory of A:\

File not found

A:\>dir c:*.let

 Volume in drive C is 486SLC25
 Volume Serial Number is 0DEZ-160A
 Directory of C:\

SEMINAR  LET          997 09-17-92   6:52a
        1 file(s)              997 bytes
                       37,371,904 bytes free

A:\>
```

5. Clear the screen.

Quick Reference   Command: MOVE (external)
MOVE Command   Syntax: move *source destination*
                         Purpose: Moves one or more files to a different drive or directory

---

RENAMING FILES (REN)

You change the name of a disk file using the REN command. The syntax
for the REN command follows:

REN *oldname newname*

You cannot, however, change the location and the name of a file at the same time. Review the following examples:

valid   `REN oldfile.bak newfile.bak`
invalid   `REN a:oldfile.bak c:newfile.bak`

The second example is invalid because it attempts to change the drive location at the same time that it changes the name of the file. To accomplish this procedure, you use the MOVE command instead.

Perform the following steps to practice using the REN command.

1. Ensure that the A:\> system prompt is displayed.

2. To rename the EXAMPLE.BAK file to EXAMPLE.OLD:
    TYPE: `ren example.bak example.old`
    PRESS: [Enter]

3. To list the files that have EXAMPLE as the file name:
    TYPE: `dir example.*`
    PRESS: [Enter]
    You should see the EXAMPLE.TXT file and an EXAMPLE.OLD file in the directory listing.

CAUTION: You should perform a DIR command after each file management operation to ensure that DOS completed the task correctly. In most cases, DOS does not provide feedback for commands entered at the system prompt.

....

Quick Reference   Command: REN (internal)
REN Command   Syntax: ren *oldname newname*
                      Purpose: Changes the name of one or more files

....

DELETING FILES (DEL)

The DEL command removes a file or files from the hard disk or a floppy diskette. The syntax for the DEL command follows:

DEL *file specification*, or
ERASE *file specification*

To practice deleting files, perform the following steps.

1. In the next section, you learn how to recover some of the files that you delete in the following steps. To ensure that you are using the standard level of protection for accidental deletions, enter the following:
   TYPE: `undelete /unload`
   PRESS: (Enter)
   This command unloads any advanced deletion tracking schemes that have been installed on your computer. If you did not have any deletion tracking schemes loaded, you will see the message "Cannot unload. UNDELETE not already resident."

   (*Note*: You would not normally perform this step before deleting or undeleting files. This step simply ensures that your computer behaves consistently with the following steps and descriptions.)

2. To delete the EXAMPLE.OLD file:
   TYPE: `del example.old`
   PRESS: (Enter)

3. TYPE: `dir example.*`
   PRESS: (Enter)
   Notice that the EXAMPLE.OLD file is no longer shown in the listing.

4. To delete the file copied to the hard disk in the Copying Files section:
   TYPE: `del c:example.bak`
   PRESS: (Enter)

5. To return the file moved to the hard disk in the Moving Files section:
   TYPE: `move c:seminar.let a:`
   PRESS: (Enter)

6. For further practice, let's create backup copies of the WK1 files:
   TYPE: `copy *.wk1 *.123`
   PRESS: (Enter)
   (*Note*: The extension of 123 refers to the originating program, Lotus 1-2-3. If you consistently use BAK for the extension on backup files, you may unknowingly mix files and forget their true extensions.)

7. TYPE: `dir /oe /w`
   PRESS: (Enter)
   You should see several files with the extension WK1 and 123.

8. To delete these backup files and free up some storage space:
   TYPE: del *.123
   PRESS: (Enter)

   CAUTION: The command del *.* is the only situation where DOS prompts you for confirmation before deleting all the files in the current directory. Therefore, be careful with other uses of wildcards with the DEL command.

9. TYPE: dir /oe /w
   PRESS: (Enter)
   There should be no files with the extension 123 in the directory listing.

Quick Reference   Command: DEL (internal)
DEL Command   Syntax: del *file specification*
                          Purpose: Deletes one or more files

UNDELETING FILES (UNDELETE)

When you delete a file, DOS places a special delete code into the first character of the file's directory entry. By default, the DEL command also removes the file from the File Allocation Table (FAT) or disk index, but does not actually erase the data from the disk. If you save a new file in the same directory, however, DOS stores the data in the first available entry marked with the special delete code. Therefore, you must undelete a file immediately after its deletion to prevent a new file from permanently overwriting its data. This is the standard level of protection provided by DOS.

For greater security, the Undelete program provides the Delete Sentry and the Delete Tracker protection schemes. The Delete Sentry offers the best protection by creating a hidden directory (named SENTRY) and copying files that you delete into that directory. To undelete a file protected by the Delete Sentry, you use the Undelete program to copy the file back to its original location. An intermediate level of protection is provided by the Delete Tracker, which uses a hidden file (PCTRACKER.DEL) to record the name and location of each file that you delete. To undelete a file protected by the Delete Tracker, you use the Undelete program to retrieve the file's complete name (including its first character) from the hidden file.

If the file's data has not been overwritten by a new file, it is fully recoverable.

By default, MS-DOS 6 provides the standard level of protection for accidentally deleted files. To load the Delete Sentry or Delete Tracker protection schemes, you use the following command syntax:

UNDELETE /S[*drive*]	Loads the Undelete program into memory and engages the Delete Sentry for the specified drive. If the drive is omitted, the Delete Sentry protects the current drive only.
UNDELETE /T*drive*	Loads the Undelete program into memory and installs the deletion-tracking system for the specified drive.
UNDELETE /STATUS	Displays the current level of protection.

To restore a file that has been accidentally deleted (regardless of the current level of protection), you execute the UNDELETE command using the following syntax:

UNDELETE *file specification* [/ALL] [/LIST]

The UNDELETE command automatically uses the highest level of protection available to recover the deleted file or files. If you use the UNDELETE command in the standard mode, you are led through each deleted file and asked to provide the first character of the files' names. To instruct DOS to restore all the deleted files in the current directory without prompting you for names, you add the /ALL switch. The /LIST switch instructs DOS to list (but not restore) the deleted files that are available for recovery.

Remember—the less time that has elapsed since the deletion, the better opportunity for a successful recovery! Let's perform the following steps.

1. To display the status of your current protection level:
   TYPE: undelete /status
   PRESS: (Enter)
   The message "UNDELETE not loaded" appears, signifying the standard level of protection. (*Remember*: You unloaded the Undelete program from memory in step 1 of the previous section's exercises.)

2. To display the list of files that are available for recovery:
TYPE: `undelete /list`
PRESS: (Enter)
The UNDELETE command checks for entries in the Delete Sentry directory, the Delete Tracker file, and finally, in the standard MS-DOS directory system. Your screen should appear similar to Figure 2.4.

Figure 2.4

List of files available for recovery using the UNDELETE command.

```
Directory: A:\
File Specifications: *.*

    Delete Sentry control file not found.

    Deletion-tracking file not found.

    MS-DOS directory contains   10 deleted files.
    Of those,  10 files may be recovered.

Using the MS-DOS directory method.

        ?ILLS    123    1939  8-08-91 12:00p  ...A
        ?UDGET   123    2771  8-08-91 12:00p  ...A
        ?MPLOYEE 123    2807  8-11-92  2:28p  ...A
        ?NCOME   123    3718  8-08-91 12:00p  ...A
        ?1       123    2258  8-08-91 12:00p  ...A
        ?2       123    2258  8-08-91 12:00p  ...A
        ?3       123    2259  8-08-91 12:00p  ...A
        ?4       123    2258  8-08-91 12:00p  ...A
        ?ALES    123    2655  8-08-91 12:00p  ...A
        ?UMMARY  123    2826  8-08-91 12:00p  ...A


A:\>
```

Notice that the recoverable files are listed with their file names and extensions. Because the first letter in each file name is missing, you must be prepared to type in the correct letter when undeleting the files.

3. To undelete INCOME.123:
TYPE: `undelete income.123`
PRESS: (Enter)

4. When prompted to proceed with the recovery, answer yes:
TYPE: `y`

5. To undelete INCOME.123, enter the first letter of the file name:
TYPE: `i`
You should see the message "File successfully undeleted."

6. To prove that the file has been restored:
   TYPE: `dir *.123`
   PRESS: [Enter]
   (*Note*: To undelete all the files appearing in the list, you would type "undelete /all" at the system prompt. Because the Undelete program cannot retrieve the first character in a deleted file's name, a # is substituted for the first character.)

7. Clear the screen.

Quick Reference *UNDELETE* *Command*	Command:	UNDELETE (external)
	Syntax:	undelete [/unload] [/s[*drive*]] [/t*drive*]
		undelete [*file specification*] [/all] [/list]
	Purpose:	Sets up the Undelete program's level of protection and restores one or more files

---

VIEWING THE CONTENTS OF A FILE (TYPE)

Most data files are created and saved to a disk using an application software program. These files are called formatted data files because the information is saved in a format that is often unique to the software programs used to create them. An unformatted data file is a plain text file that adheres to the **ASCII** (American Standard Code for Information Interchange) standards. These files often have the extension TXT, ASC, or BAT. Any computer with DOS can display an ASCII text file using the DOS TYPE command. You cannot display a WordPerfect, Lotus, Word, or Excel file using TYPE. The syntax for the command follows:

TYPE *file name*

Perform the following steps from the A:\> system prompt.

1. TYPE: `type example.txt`
   PRESS: [Enter]
   (*Note*: To produce a printed copy of this file, you press [Ctrl]+[PrtScr] to turn on continuous printing, enter the above TYPE command, and then press [Ctrl]+[PrtScr] to turn off continuous printing.)

2. TYPE: `type income.wk1`
    PRESS: (Enter)
    Your screen should now appear similar to Figure 2.5. Note that the file is not readable. A WK1 file is created and saved in a special worksheet format using Lotus 1-2-3. In other words, this file is a formatted data file, not an ASCII text file.

Figure 2.5

Viewing the contents of formatted and unformatted files.

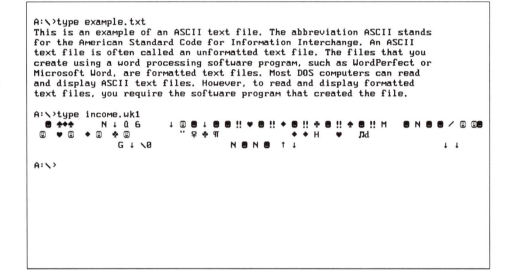

```
A:\>type example.txt
This is an example of an ASCII text file. The abbreviation ASCII stands
for the American Standard Code for Information Interchange. An ASCII
text file is often called an unformatted text file. The files that you
create using a word processing software program, such as WordPerfect or
Microsoft Word, are formatted text files. Most DOS computers can read
and display ASCII text files. However, to read and display formatted
text files, you require the software program that created the file.

A:\>type income.wk1
```

Quick Reference   Command: TYPE (internal)
TYPE Command   Syntax: type *file name*
                         Purpose: Views the contents of an ASCII text file

---

DISPLAYING FILE ATTRIBUTES (ATTRIB)

As you have seen by using the DIR command, DOS keeps track of each file's name, extension, size, and its creation date and time. In addition to this standard information, each file also possesses certain **file attributes**. The boot process, for example, uses two files with hidden attributes to load parts of the operating system. These two files are hidden from a DIR listing and other file management commands to avoid accidental deletion.

You use the ATTRIB command to view and change the attributes of a file or files. The syntax for the ATTRIB command follows:

ATTRIB [+/-] [R] [A] [S] [H] [*file specification*]

Table 2.3 explains the various file attributes.

Table 2.3	*Attribute*	*Description*
File Attributes	R	Read-only attribute; allows a file to be viewed but not modified or deleted
	A	Archive attribute; provides information for backing up files
	S	System attribute; tells DOS that the file belongs to the DOS operating system files
	H	Hidden attribute; hides a file from a DIR listing and other file management commands

Perform the following steps.

1. Ensure that the A:\> system prompt is displayed.

2. View the attributes for all the files on drive A:.
   TYPE: attrib *.*
   PRESS: (Enter)

3. To view the attributes for all the WK1 files:
   TYPE: attrib *.wk1
   PRESS: (Enter)

4. To change the attributes of the WK1 files to read-only:
   TYPE: attrib +r *.wk1
   PRESS: (Enter)
   Note that you add an attribute by placing a plus sign in front of the attribute letter.

5. To change the attributes of the WK1 files to hidden:
   TYPE: `attrib +h *.wk1`
   PRESS: [Enter]

6. Perform a directory listing:
   TYPE: `dir`
   PRESS: [Enter]
   The WK1 files are no longer displayed in the directory listing.

7. To view all the files in a directory regardless of hidden attributes:
   TYPE: `dir /a`
   PRESS: [Enter]

8. To view all the files that have a read-only attribute:
   TYPE: `dir /ar`
   PRESS: [Enter]

9. To view the attributes of the WK1 files:
   TYPE: `attrib *.wk1`
   PRESS: [Enter]

10. To remove the read-only and hidden attributes for the WK1 files:
    TYPE: `attrib -r -h *.wk1`
    PRESS: [Enter]
    Note that you clear an attribute by placing a minus sign in front of the attribute letter.

....

Quick Reference	Command:	ATTRIB (external)
ATTRIB	Syntax:	attrib [+/-] [r] [a] [s] [h] *file name*
Command		r Read-only
		a Archive
		s System
		h Hidden
	Purpose:	Views and changes the attributes of one or more files

....

USING THE DOS SHELL

This section introduces the DOS Shell procedures for managing files on hard disks and floppy diskettes. In addition, you explore methods for selecting files and customizing the Shell's appearance.

CUSTOMIZING THE DISPLAY

Along with being able to change the color and screen mode, you select the areas you want displayed in the DOS Shell. For example, if you don't want to use the Shell for launching application software programs, you can remove the Program List area from the screen. This section shows you how you accomplish this and other methods for changing the appearance of the DOS Shell.

CHANGING THE SCREEN COLOR.   To change the color of the screen, choose the Options, Colors command from the Menu bar. A dialog box appears with eight predefined color settings contained in a list box. You use the cursor-movement keys or the mouse to highlight a color choice and then select the OK command button. You can also select the Preview button to view the color setting without leaving the dialog box. To return to the Shell without making any changes, select the Cancel command button.

Perform the following steps.

1.   Ensure that the A:\> system prompt is displayed.

2.   Load the DOS Shell program:
     TYPE: `dosshell`
     PRESS: (Enter)

3.   To change the color of the DOS Shell screen:
     CHOOSE: Options, Colors
     A dialog box appears as shown in Figure 2.6.

Figure 2.6

The Options,
Colors dialog box.

```
┌──────────────────────────────────────────────────────────────────┐
│                          MS-DOS Shell                              │
│  File  Options  View  Tree  Help                                   │
│ A:\                                                                │
│ ▣A   ▣B   ▢C   ▢H                                                  │
│                                                                    │
│      Directory Tree                      A:\*.*                    │
│   ┌─ A:\     ┌────────── Color Scheme ──────────┐ 1,939  08-08-91 ▲│
│             │                                    │   897  08-31-92  │
│             │ Current Scheme: Monochrome-4 Colors│ 2,771  08-08-91  │
│             │  Basic Blue                      ▲ │ 6,265  08-31-92  │
│             │  Ocean                             │ 2,290  11-09-92  │
│             │  Monochrome-2 Colors               │ 2,807  08-11-92  │
│             │  Monochrome-4 Colors               │   500  10-26-92  │
│             │  Reverse                         ▼ │ 8,994  11-09-92  │
│             │                                    │ 5,150  08-31-92  │
│             │  ┌─ OK ─┐  ┌─ Preview ─┐ ┌ Cancel ┐│ 1,440  10-29-92  │
│             │  └──────┘  └───────────┘ └────────┘│ 1,440  10-29-92  │
│             └────────────────┤ ▤ INCOME  .123    │ 3,718  08-08-91 ▼│
│                              Main                                   │
│   ☐  Command Prompt                                              ▲ │
│   ☐  Editor                                                        │
│   ☐  MS-DOS QBasic                                                 │
│   ▦  Disk Utilities                                                │
│                                                                    │
│                                                                  ▼ │
│ F10=Actions  Shift+F9=Command Prompt                        9:06p  │
└──────────────────────────────────────────────────────────────────┘
```

4. SELECT: Emerald City option

5. CLICK: Preview command button
   Your screen changes to the highlighted color setting. (*Note*: If you do
   not have a mouse, you execute the CLICK instruction by moving to the
   command button using [Tab] and pressing [Enter].)

6. SELECT: Turquoise color option
   CLICK: Preview command button

7. Select and preview the other color combinations and then choose the
   option that you prefer before continuing.

8. CLICK: OK command button
   By selecting the OK command button, the highlighted option becomes
   the default color setting for the current and all subsequent sessions.

Quick Reference
*Changing the
Screen Color of
the DOS Shell*
1. CHOOSE: Options, Colors
2. SELECT: *a color setting* from the list box
3. a. CLICK: OK to use the new color setting
   b. CLICK: Preview to temporarily view the highlighted color setting
   c. CLICK: Cancel to return to the DOS Shell without any changes

CHANGING THE SCREEN MODE.   You can work with the DOS Shell using a Text or Graphics screen mode. Although the **Text mode** may respond quicker to commands, the **Graphics mode** provides a smoother mouse interface. The various screen modes also affect the amount of information that appears on the screen. To change the screen mode, choose the Options, Display command from the Menu bar. A dialog box appears with several Text and Graphics mode options, depending on your computer's graphic capabilities. Use the cursor-movement keys or the mouse to highlight your screen mode choice and then select the OK command button. You can also select the Preview button to view the screen mode without leaving the dialog box. To return to the Shell without making any changes, select the Cancel command button.

Perform the following steps.

1. To change the screen mode for the DOS Shell:
    CHOOSE: Options, Display

2. The options appearing in the list box reflect your computer's ability to display graphics. To view the highest resolution available for graphics:
    SELECT: *the last option at the bottom of the dialog box*
    On some computers, this command enables you to display up to 60 lines on a screen, whereas the normal text mode is 25 lines per screen.

3. CLICK: Preview command button

4. Select and preview the other screen modes and then choose the option that you prefer before continuing.

5. CLICK: OK
    By selecting OK, you make the highlighted option the default screen mode setting for the current and all subsequent sessions.

Quick Reference
*Changing the
Screen Mode of
the DOS Shell*

1. CHOOSE: Options, Display
2. SELECT: *a screen mode* from the list box.
3. a. CLICK: OK to use the new mode setting
   b. CLICK: Preview to temporarily view the highlighted mode setting
   c. CLICK: Cancel to return to the DOS Shell without any changes

---

SELECTING THE VIEW.   In the first session, you were introduced to several areas that appear in the DOS Shell, including the Directory Tree area, File List area, Program List area, and the Active Task List area. The View option on the Menu bar enables you to display or hide these areas of the DOS Shell. There are five commands available under the View option, as described in Table 2.4.

Table 2.4

View Commands

Command	*Description*
Single File List	Displays the Directory Tree and the File List area
Dual File Lists	Displays two Directory Trees and two File List areas
All Files	Displays all the files on the current drive, regardless of the directory structure
Program/File Lists	Displays the Directory Tree, File List, Program List, and Active Task List areas (the default view)
Program List	Displays the Program List and Active Task List areas

---

Perform the following steps.

1. To view the directory structure and files for the current drive:
   CHOOSE: View, Single File List

2. To view the directory structure and files for both drive A: and drive C:, choose the following command:
   CHOOSE: View, Dual File Lists
   SELECT: drive C: icon in the bottom window

3. To view file information only:
   CHOOSE: View, All Files

Your screen should appear similar to Figure 2.7.

Figure 2.7

The <u>V</u>iew, <u>A</u>ll Files command.

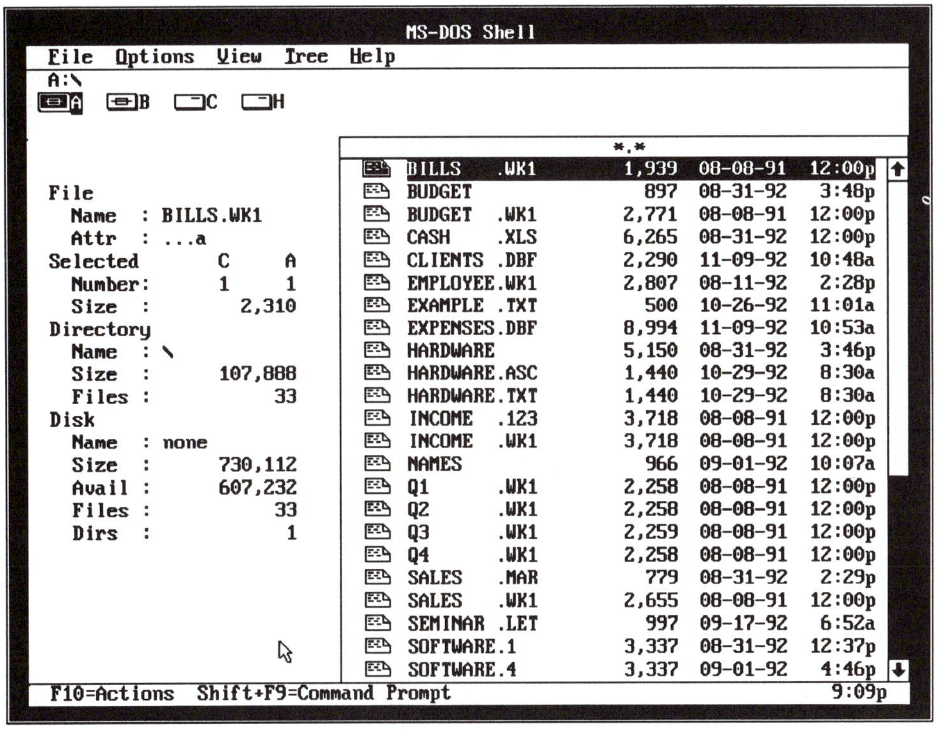

```
                                      MS-DOS Shell
    File   Options   View   Tree   Help
    A:\
    ▭A   ▭B   ▭C   ▭H

                                          *.*
                          ▤  BILLS    .WK1     1,939  08-08-91   12:00p ↑
    File                  ▤  BUDGET              897  08-31-92    3:48p
      Name  : BILLS.WK1   ▤  BUDGET   .WK1     2,771  08-08-91   12:00p
      Attr  : ...a        ▤  CASH     .XLS     6,265  08-31-92   12:00p
    Selected      C    A  ▤  CLIENTS  .DBF     2,290  11-09-92   10:48a
      Number:     1    1  ▤  EMPLOYEE .WK1     2,807  08-11-92    2:28p
      Size  :   2,310    ▤  EXAMPLE  .TXT       500  10-26-92   11:01a
    Directory             ▤  EXPENSES .DBF     8,994  11-09-92   10:53a
      Name  : \           ▤  HARDWARE          5,150  08-31-92    3:46p
      Size  :   107,888   ▤  HARDWARE .ASC     1,440  10-29-92    8:30a
      Files :        33   ▤  HARDWARE .TXT     1,440  10-29-92    8:30a
    Disk                  ▤  INCOME   .123     3,718  08-08-91   12:00p
      Name  : none        ▤  INCOME   .WK1     3,718  08-08-91   12:00p
      Size  :   730,112   ▤  NAMES              966  09-01-92   10:07a
      Avail :   607,232   ▤  Q1       .WK1     2,258  08-08-91   12:00p
      Files :        33   ▤  Q2       .WK1     2,258  08-08-91   12:00p
      Dirs  :         1   ▤  Q3       .WK1     2,259  08-08-91   12:00p
                          ▤  Q4       .WK1     2,258  08-08-91   12:00p
                          ▤  SALES    .MAR       779  08-31-92    2:29p
                          ▤  SALES    .WK1     2,655  08-08-91   12:00p
                          ▤  SEMINAR  .LET       997  09-17-92    6:52a
                   �k      ▤  SOFTWARE .1       3,337  08-31-92   12:37p
                          ▤  SOFTWARE .4       3,337  09-01-92    4:46p ↓
    F10=Actions   Shift+F9=Command Prompt                        9:09p
```

4. To return to the default view:
   CHOOSE: <u>V</u>iew, Program/<u>F</u>ile Lists

....

Quick Reference
Specifying the Areas to View in the DOS Shell

CHOOSE: <u>V</u>iew, *command*, where *command* is one of the following:
- <u>S</u>ingle File List   Displays Directory Tree and File List areas
- <u>D</u>ual File Lists   Displays two Directory Trees and File Lists
- <u>A</u>ll Files   Displays all files from the current drive
- Program/<u>F</u>ile Lists   Displays the default view
- <u>P</u>rogram List   Displays Program List and Active Task List

....

SELECTING FILES

The DOS Shell provides keyboard and mouse methods for selecting a file or a group of files. The file specification appears in the Title bar of the File List area. When you first load the DOS Shell, the file specification is *.*

and is preceded with the current drive letter (for example, A: or C:). The *.* specification matches all files in the current directory.

LIMITING THE DISPLAY OF FILES.   To limit the display of files in the File List area, you choose the Options, File Display Options command from the Menu bar. In the dialog box, enter a file specification and choose a sort order for the files. Select the OK command button to save the changes and return to the DOS Shell. Select the Cancel button to return to the Shell without making any changes.

Perform the following steps.

1. To ensure that you have drive A: selected, perform the following keyboard shortcut:
    PRESS: Ctrl+a

2. Change the view to display a single file list:
    CHOOSE: View, Single File List

3. To limit the File List area to displaying WK1 files only:
    CHOOSE: Options, File Display Options

4. Enter the WK1 file specification:
    TYPE: *.wk1
    PRESS: Enter
    The File List area now shows only WK1 files. As well, the Title bar reads A:*.WK1. This command is similar to entering dir *.wk1 from the command line.

5. To sort the files by size in the File List area:
    CHOOSE: Options, File Display Options

6. SELECT: Size option button in the Sort by group
    You use the Tab and Shift+Tab combination to move through the dialog box using the keyboard. With a mouse, simply click on the option button.

7. PRESS: Enter or CLICK: OK

8. To display all the files sorted by name:
    CHOOSE: Options, File Display Options
    TYPE: *.*
    SELECT: Name option button
    PRESS: Enter

SELECTING FILES USING THE KEYBOARD. The DOS Shell is based on a "Select" and then "Do" methodology, where you highlight the desired files and then execute the appropriate command. To select files using the keyboard, you must first make the File List area active. In other words, you press [Tab] and [Shift]+[Tab] to cycle through the areas in the DOS Shell until the Title bar for the File List area is highlighted.

The primary methods for selecting files using the keyboard include:

1. *Selecting a single file.*
   To select a single file, position the Selection cursor over the file using the cursor-movement keys. Press the [Home] key to move to the first file and press the [End] key to move to the last file in the list. A file is selected when it appears in reverse video.

2. *Selecting a group of contiguous files.*
   To select a group of files that are contiguous (next to each other) in the File List area, position the Selection cursor on the first file, hold down the [Shift] key, and then press the [↓] key to highlight each additional file. When you are finished selecting files, release the [Shift] key.

3. *Selecting a group of contiguous files using the Add mode.*
   To select a group of contiguous files using the **Add mode**, position the Selection cursor on the first file and then press [Shift]+[F8] to invoke the Add mode. The word "Add" appears on the Status bar. Position the highlight bar on the last file in the group and press [Shift]+Space Bar. All the files between the first and last file are selected. Press [Shift]+[F8] to turn off the Add mode.

4. *Selecting a group of noncontiguous files using the Add mode.*
   To select a group of noncontiguous files using the Add mode, position the Selection cursor on the first file and then press [Shift]+[F8] to invoke the Add mode. Position the Selection cursor on each additional file and press the Space Bar to select. Once all the files are selected, press [Shift]+[F8] to turn off the Add mode.

5. *Selecting all of the files.*
   To select all of the files in the File List area, you press Ctrl+/. You may also choose the File, Select All command.

6. *Removing the selection.*
   To remove the highlighting from files in the File List area, you press Ctrl+\. You may also choose the File, Deselect All command.

SELECTING FILES USING A MOUSE.   The primary methods available for selecting files using a mouse include:

1. *Selecting a single file.*
   To select a single file, position the mouse pointer over the file and click the left mouse button once.

2. *Selecting a group of contiguous files.*
   To select a group of contiguous files, position the mouse pointer over the first file and click the left mouse button once to select the file. Then position the mouse pointer over the last file in the group, hold down the Shift key, and click once. All the files between the first and last file are selected. Once the files are highlighted, release the Shift key.

3. *Selecting a group of noncontiguous files.*
   To select a group of noncontiguous files, position the mouse pointer over the first file and click the left mouse button once to select the file. Position the mouse pointer on each additional file, hold down the Ctrl key, and click once to select. Repeat this Ctrl+click sequence until all the desired files are selected, and then release the Ctrl key.

Perform the following steps to practice selecting files using the keyboard and mouse methods.

1. Select the File List area by pressing Tab until its Title bar is highlighted.

2. To move to the end of the file list:
   PRESS: End
   The highlight bar moves to the last file in the list.

3. To move to the beginning of the list:
   PRESS: Home

4. To select the first five files in the list using the keyboard:
   PRESS: [Shift] and hold it down
   PRESS: [↓] four times
   The first five files are highlighted.

5. Release the [Shift] key.

6. To select the first five files in the list using a mouse:
   PRESS: [Home] to move to the first file in the list
   PRESS: [Shift] and hold it down
   CLICK: the fifth file in the list

7. Release the [Shift] key.

8. To select three noncontiguous files using the keyboard:
   PRESS: [Home] to remove the previous selection
   PRESS: [Shift]+[F8] to turn on the Add mode
   Notice that the word "Add" appears on the Status bar.

9. PRESS: [↓] three times
   PRESS: Space Bar to select the file
   Notice that the first file in the list remains highlighted.

10. PRESS: [↓] twice
    PRESS: Space Bar to select the file
    PRESS: [Shift]+[F8] to turn off the Add mode
    Your screen should now appear similar to Figure 2.8. (*Note*: The files that you have highlighted may differ from the file names in the example.)

Figure 2.8

Selecting multiple
files using the
keyboard.

```
╔══════════════════════════════════════════════════════════════╗
║                         MS-DOS Shell                           ║
║ File   Options   View   Tree   Help                            ║
║ A:\                                                            ║
║ ▣A    ▣B    ▭C    ▭H                                         ║
║ ┌──── Directory Tree ──────┐  ┌──────── A:\*.* ──────────────┐ ║
║ ┌ A:\              ┃↑┃        ▤ BILLS    .WK1    1,939  08-08-91 ↑║
║                              ▤ BUDGET             897  08-31-92  ║
║                              ▤ BUDGET   .WK1    2,771  08-08-91  ║
║                              ▣ CASH     .XLS    6,265  08-31-92  ║
║                              ▤ CLIENTS  .DBF    2,290  11-09-92  ║
║                              ▣ EMPLOYEE .WK1    2,807  08-11-92  ║
║                              ▤ EXAMPLE  .TXT      500  10-26-92  ║
║                              ▤ EXPENSES .DBF    8,994  11-09-92  ║
║                              ▤ HARDWARE         5,150  08-31-92  ║
║                              ▤ HARDWARE .ASC    1,440  10-29-92  ║
║                              ▤ HARDWARE .TXT    1,440  10-29-92  ║
║                              ▤ INCOME   .123    3,718  08-08-91  ║
║                              ▤ INCOME   .WK1    3,718  08-08-91  ║
║                              ▤ NAMES             966  09-01-92  ║
║                              ▤ Q1       .WK1    2,258  08-08-91  ║
║                              ▤ Q2       .WK1    2,258  08-08-91  ║
║                              ▤ Q3       .WK1    2,259  08-08-91  ║
║                              ▤ Q4       .WK1    2,258  08-08-91  ║
║                              ▤ SALES    .MAR      779  08-31-92  ║
║                              ▤ SALES    .WK1    2,655  08-08-91  ║
║                              ▤ SEMINAR  .LET      997  09-17-92  ║
║                              ▤ SOFTWARE .1      3,337  08-31-92  ║
║                      ┃↓┃     ▤ SOFTWARE .4      3,337  09-01-92 ↓║
║ F10=Actions  Shift+F9=Command Prompt                    9:15p  ║
╚══════════════════════════════════════════════════════════════╝
```

11. PRESS: [Home] to remove the previous selection

12. To select five noncontiguous files using a mouse:
    CLICK: *on a single file*

13. PRESS: [Ctrl] and hold it down
    CLICK: *on four additional files anywhere in the File List area*

14. To remove the highlighting, release the [Ctrl] key and then click on any
    one file in the File List area.

....

Quick Reference   1. Position the highlight bar on the first file to select.
Selecting Files   2. PRESS: [Shift]+[F8] to invoke the Add mode
Using the   3. Position the highlight bar on each additional file to include.
Keyboard   4. PRESS: Space Bar to select
                           5. PRESS: [Shift]+[F8] to turn off the Add mode

....

....

Quick Reference 1. Click the mouse pointer on the first file to select.
Selecting Files 2. PRESS: Ctrl and hold it down
Using a Mouse 3. Click the mouse pointer on each additional file to include.
  4. Release the Ctrl key.

....

COPYING AND MOVING FILES

To copy files using the DOS Shell, you first select the desired files from the File List area and then issue the File, Copy command. When prompted by the dialog box, you enter the target or destination for the selected files. To move files from one location to another, you choose the File, Move command from the Menu bar. The only difference between Copy and Move is that with Move the original files are deleted.

The DOS Shell offers a shortcut for copying and moving files called drag and drop. After selecting files from the File List area, you simply drag the highlighted files to their new location (for example, a folder in the Directory Tree area or an icon in the Drives area). If you drag the files to a different directory on the same disk drive, DOS views the mouse action as a Move command. If you drag the files to a different drive, DOS views the mouse action as a Copy command.

Perform the following steps to practice copying and moving files using the menu commands and the drag and drop feature.

1. Select a view that shows two Directory Trees and File List areas:
   CHOOSE: View, Dual File Lists

2. Display the files for drive A: in the top window and the files for drive C: in the bottom window. Make sure that you select the root directory folder in the drive C: window. Your screen should appear similar to Figure 2.9 before continuing. (*Note*: Your screen display may show different file names than the screen graphic in Figure 2.9.)

Figure 2.9

Viewing files from
drive A: and
drive C: at the
same time.

```
                              MS-DOS Shell
    File  Options  View  Tree  Help
    A:\
    [=]A   [=]B   []C   []H
              Directory Tree                          A:\*.*
    [] A:\                              ↑    [] BILLS    .WK1      1,939   08-08-91  ↑
                                             [] BUDGET               897   08-31-92
                                             [] BUDGET   .WK1      2,771   08-08-91
                                             [] CASH     .XLS      6,265   08-31-92
                                             [] CLIENTS  .DBF      2,290   11-09-92
                                             [] EMPLOYEE .WK1      2,807   08-11-92
                                             [] EXAMPLE  .TXT        500   10-26-92
                                             [] EXPENSES .DBF      8,994   11-09-92
                                             [] HARDWARE           5,150   08-31-92
                                      ↓      [] HARDWARE.ASC       1,440   10-29-92  ↓

    [=]A   [=]B   [=]C   []H
              Directory Tree                          C:\*.*
    [] C:\                              ↑    [] AUTOEXEC.BAT        371   03-18-94   ↑
        [+] ASCEND                           [] COMMAND  .COM    54,619   09-30-93
        [+] COMM                             [] CONFIG   .SYS       569   03-12-94
        [+] CSERVE                           [] EXAMPLE  .BAK       500   10-26-92
        [+] DATA                             [] WINA20   .386     9,349   09-30-93
        [] DOS
        [+] EXCEL
        [+] GRAPHICS
        [] MYOB                        ↓                                           ↓
    F10=Actions   Shift+F9=Command Prompt                               9:17p
```

3. SELECT: the File List area for drive A:

4. SELECT: BUDGET.WK1 file

5. To copy the BUDGET.WK1 file to the root directory of drive C:,
    choose the following:
    CHOOSE: File, Copy
    (*Note*: You can also press [F8] to execute the File, Copy command.)

6. Enter the destination for the file in the dialog box:
    TYPE: c:
    PRESS: [Enter]
    The BUDGET.WK1 file appears in the File List area for drive C:.

7. To move the CLIENTS.DBF file to drive C:, do the following:
    SELECT: CLIENTS.DBF file in the drive A: File List area
    CHOOSE: File, Move
    Your screen should appear similar to Figure 2.10. (*Note*: You can also
    press [F7] to execute the File, Move command.)

Figure 2.10

Moving the
CLIENTS.DBF file
from drive A: to
drive C:.

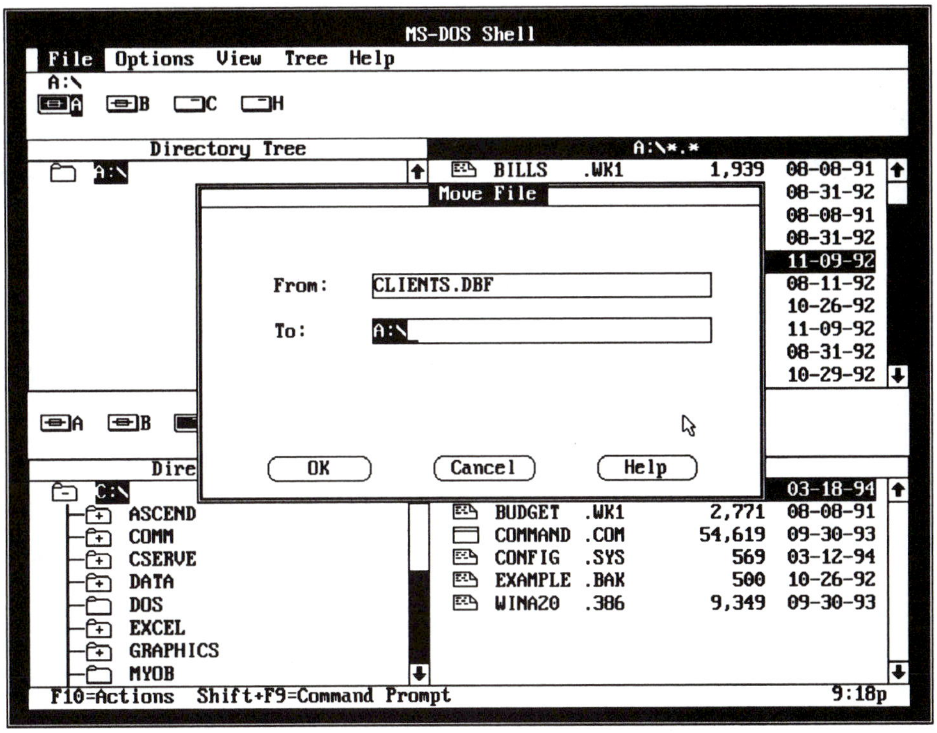

8. Enter the destination for the file in the dialog box:
   TYPE: c:
   PRESS: [Enter]
   The CLIENTS.DBF file appears in the File List area for drive C: and is removed from the drive A: File List area.

9. To copy multiple files using the drag and drop method, first select the files from the drive A: File List area using the mouse:
   CLICK: EMPLOYEE.WK1
   PRESS: [Ctrl] and hold it down
   CLICK: HARDWARE
   CLICK: INCOME.WK1

10. Release the [Ctrl] key. The files remain highlighted in reverse video.

11. Position the mouse pointer over one of the highlighted files.

12. CLICK: left mouse button and hold it down

13. DRAG: mouse pointer to the root directory folder for drive C:
    Position the mouse pointer directly over the folder appearing to the left of the C:\ label. (*Note*: You can also drop the files on the drive C: icon in the Drive area. However, the files are copied or moved to the default directory on the drive, which may not be the desired directory. Therefore, you should drop files directly on the target directory folder in a drive, rather than on a drive icon.)

14. Release the mouse button.

15. If the mouse pointer was positioned correctly, a dialog box appears asking you for confirmation to copy the files to drive C:. Answer yes:
    PRESS: [Enter] or CLICK: Yes

    CAUTION: Ensure that the wording in the dialog box is correct before responding to the prompt. For example, check that the dialog box confirms a copy or move operation and that the target location is accurate. There is no UNDO command available in the DOS Shell.

Quick Reference   1. Select the files to copy or move.
Copying and   2. CHOOSE: File, Copy or File, Move
Moving Files   3. Enter the destination into the dialog box.
                         4. PRESS: [Enter] or CLICK: OK

RENAMING FILES

To rename files using the DOS Shell, you first select the desired file from the File List area and then issue the File, Rename command. When prompted by the dialog box, you enter the new name for the selected file.

Perform the following steps.

1. SELECT: the File List area for drive C:

2. SELECT: BUDGET.WK1 file
   Make certain that you are selecting the file from the File List area for drive C:, and not drive A:.

3. To rename the file as BUDGET.123:
   CHOOSE: File, Rename

4. Enter the new name in the dialog box:
    TYPE: budget.123
    PRESS: [Enter]
    The new file name appears in the File List area.

....

Quick Reference   1. Select the file or files to rename.
Renaming Files   2. CHOOSE: File, Rename
                        3. Enter the new name into the dialog box.
                        4. PRESS: [Enter] or CLICK: OK

....

DELETING FILES

To delete files using the DOS Shell, you first select the desired files from the File List area and then issue the File, Delete command. When prompted by the dialog box, you confirm each deletion by pressing [Enter] or clicking the Yes command button. If you need to delete many files at once, the confirmation of each individual file can become quite tedious. Fortunately, you can turn off this safety feature using the Options, Confirmation command. When executed, the command gives you a dialog box, as shown in Figure 2.11. To turn off the Confirm on Delete option, you remove the × mark from the check box. For this section, however, let's leave the Confirm on Delete check box selected.

Figure 2.11

The Options, Confirmation dialog box.

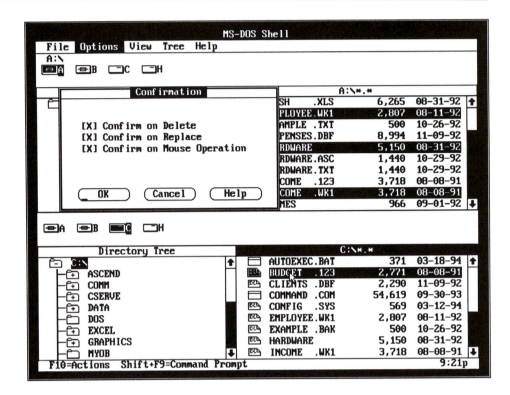

Perform the following steps.

1. SELECT: the File List area for drive C:

2. SELECT: HARDWARE file

3. To delete the file:
   CHOOSE: File, Delete
   PRESS: [Enter] or CLICK: Yes

4. CHOOSE: Options, File Display Options
   TYPE: *.wk1
   PRESS: [Enter]

5. To delete all the WK1 files:
   PRESS: [Ctrl]+/
   PRESS: [Delete]
   Notice that the shortcut keystroke for the File, Delete command is the [Delete] key.

6. To proceed with the deletion:
   PRESS: [Enter] or CLICK: OK

7. Since the Confirm on Delete option is selected, you must confirm the deletion for each selected file:
PRESS: (Enter) or CLICK: Yes

8. Continue confirming the deletion of the selected files.

9. CHOOSE: Options, File Display Options
TYPE: * . *
PRESS: (Enter)

10. To delete the files copied to the hard disk from the Advantage Diskette:
SELECT: BUDGET.123 in the File List area
PRESS: (Ctrl) and hold it down
CLICK: CLIENTS.DBF
Both files are highlighted in the File List area.

11. PRESS: (Delete)
PRESS: (Enter) multiple times to confirm the deletion of both files

12. CHOOSE: View, Program/File List

....

Quick Reference   1. Select the file or files to delete.
Deleting Files   2. CHOOSE: File, Delete, or
        PRESS: (Delete)
        3. PRESS: (Enter) to confirm the deletion

....

UNDELETING FILES

You restore files that have been accidentally deleted using the UNDELETE command. In the DOS Shell, the UNDELETE command is located under the Disk Utilities group in the Program List area. To display the program items available under the Disk Utilities group, you highlight the option and press (Enter) or you double-click the mouse pointer on the item. The Undelete program item appearing in the Disk Utilities group is identical to the UNDELETE command entered at the system prompt.

After you choose the Undelete program item, the dialog box in Figure 2.12 appears. To list the recently deleted files, leave the default parameter of /LIST in the text box and press (Enter). To restore all the files included in the deletion list, you replace the /LIST parameter with /ALL. To restore a single file or group of files from the list, enter the file specification in the dialog box and then confirm each recovery by entering the first character of the files' names. For further information and practice on restoring files, refer to the Using the Command Line section, Undeleting Files.

Figure 2.12

The Undelete
dialog box.

```
┌──────────────────────────────────────────────────────────────────┐
│                          MS-DOS Shell                              │
│  File  Options  View  Help                                         │
│ A:\                                                                │
│ ▣A   ▣B  ▢C  ▢H                                                    │
│  ┌────────────────────── Undelete ──────────────────┐ 08-08-91 ↑  │
│ 🗁 A:\│                                               │ 08-31-92    │
│      │ WARNING! This action may cause the permanent loss of│08-08-91│
│      │ some deleted files.  Press F1 for more information. │08-31-92│
│      │                                               │ 08-11-92    │
│      │ Parameters . . .   ┌/LIST_____┐     │ 10-26-92    │
│      │                    └────────────────────┘     │ 11-09-92    │
│      │ (    OK    )    ( Cancel )      ( Help )       │ 08-31-92    │
│      └─────────────────────────────────────────────┘             │
│                      📄 HARDWARE.ASC      1,440  10-29-92          │
│                      📄 HARDWARE.TXT      1,440  10-29-92          │
│                      📄 INCOME  .123      3,718  08-08-91          │
│                ↓     📄 INCOME  .WK1      3,718  08-08-91  ↓        │
│ ──────────────────────── Disk Utilities ──────────────────────    │
│  ▦ Main                                                      ↑     │
│  ▭ Disk Copy                                                       │
│  ▭ Backup Fixed Disk                                               │
│  ▭ Restore Fixed Disk                                              │
│  ▭ Quick Format                                                    │
│  ▭ Format                                                          │
│  ▣ Undelete                                                        │
│                                                              ↓     │
│ F10=Actions   Shift+F9=Command Prompt                       9:25p  │
└──────────────────────────────────────────────────────────────────┘
```

Quick Reference
Undeleting Files

1. SELECT: Disk Utilities program group
2. SELECT: Undelete program item
3. a. Enter /LIST to view the files available for recovery.
   b. Enter /ALL to restore all the files displayed by /LIST.
   c. Enter a file specification to restore a file or group of files.

VIEWING THE CONTENTS OF A FILE

To view the contents of an ASCII text file using the DOS Shell, you select the desired file from the File List area and then issue the File, View Contents command. This command has the same results as the TYPE command.

Perform the following steps.

1. Ensure that the drive A: directory structure is displayed in the Directory Tree area and that "A:*.*" appears in the File List Title bar.

2. SELECT: the File List area for drive A:

3. SELECT: EXAMPLE.TXT
    This file is an example of a text file.

4. To view the contents of the highlighted file:
    CHOOSE: File, View File Contents
    The View File Contents command displays the file in text format. (*Note*: You can also press F9 to execute the File, View File Contents command.)

5. To return to the DOS Shell:
    PRESS: Esc

6. SELECT: INCOME.WK1
    This is an example of a formatted data file created using Lotus 1-2-3.

7. To view the INCOME.WK1 file:
    CHOOSE: File, View File Contents
    The View File Contents command displays the file in a hex format because it is a formatted data file. Your screen should appear similar to Figure 2.13.

Figure 2.13

Viewing a
formatted data
file.

```
                          MS-DOS Shell - INCOME.WK1
   Display  View  Help
   ┌ To view file's content use PgUp or PgDn or ↑ or ↓.                      ┐

     000000   00000200  06040600  08000000  00004E00    . . . . . . . . . . . . . .N.
     000010   19009600  36000000  00001900  01000200    ..û.6. . . . . . . . . .
     000020   19000200  02001300  03000200  13000400    . . . . . . . . . . . . . .
     000030   02001300  05000200  13000600  02001300    . . . . . . . . . . . . . .
     000040   4D000000  02004E00  02000200  2F000100    M. . . . . .N. . . . ./. . .
     000050   01020001  00FF0300  01000004  00010000    . . . . . . . . . . . . . .
     000060   05000100  FF070020  00000000  0022000C    . . . . . .  . . . . . .".
     000070   00050014  00000000  00000000  00000000    . . . . . . . . . . . . . .
     000080   00040004  00480000  00080003  0000000E    . . . . . .H. . . . . . .
     000090   64002000  00000000  00000000  00000000    d. . . . . . . . . . . . .
     0000A0   00000000  00000000  00000000  00000000    . . . . . . . . . . . . . .
     0000B0   00000000  47001900  5C300000  00000000    . . . .G. . .\0. . . . . .
     0000C0   00000000  00000000  4E000200  4E000200    . . . . . . . .N. . .N. . .
     0000D0   00180019  0000FFFF  0000FFFF  0000FFFF    . . . . . .  . . . ..
     0000E0   0000FFFF  0000FFFF  0000FFFF  00001900    . . . ..  . . . . . ..
     0000F0   1900FFFF  0000FFFF  0000FFFF  0000FFFF    . . . . . . . . . . ..
     000100   0000FFFF  0000FFFF  0000001A  000800FF    . . . . . .  . . . . . .
     000110   FF0000FF  FF000030  00010000  1C000800    . .  . .0. . . . . . . .
     000120   FFFF0000  FFFF0000  1B000800  FFFF0000    . . . .  . . . . . ..
     000130   FFFF0000  1D000900  FFFF0000  FFFF0000    . . . . . .  . . . ..
     000140   00230009  00FFFF00  00FFFF00  00006700    .#. . . . .  . . . ...g.
     000150   1900FFFF  0000FFFF  0000FFFF  0000FFFF    . . . . . .  . . . ..
     000160   0000FFFF  0000FFFF  00000069  002800FF    . .  . .  . . .i.(.
     000170   FF0000FF  FF0000FF  FF0000FF  FF0000FF    . .  . .  . .  . .
     000180   FF0000FF  FF0000FF  FF0000FF  FF0000FF    . .  . .  . .  . .
   └ ↵=PageDown   Esc=Cancel   F9=Hex/ASCII                              9:28p ┘
```

8. To return to the DOS Shell:
    PRESS: (Esc)

As shown above, an ASCII text file is viewed using a **text format**, while a
formatted data file is viewed using a **hex format**. The <u>V</u>iew File Contents
command is rarely useful for viewing formatted data files.

. . . .

Quick Reference   1. Select the file to view.
Viewing the   2. CHOOSE: <u>F</u>ile, <u>V</u>iew File Contents
Contents of a File   3. Use the cursor-movement keys or mouse to move through the file.

. . . .

CHANGING THE FILE ATTRIBUTES

To change the attributes for files using the DOS Shell, you select the
desired file or files from the File List area and then issue the <u>F</u>ile, <u>C</u>hange
Attributes command. This command is the DOS Shell version of the
ATTRIB command. Refer to Table 2.3 for a description of the available file
attributes.

Perform the following steps.

1. SELECT: the File List area for drive A:

2. SELECT: EXAMPLE.TXT

3. To change the attributes of the highlighted file so that it can be viewed but not modified:
   CHOOSE: File, Change Attributes
   The Change Attributes dialog box appears.

4. To set the read-only attribute using the mouse:
   SELECT: Read-only
   CLICK: OK

5. To remove the read-only attribute using the keyboard:
   CHOOSE: File, Change Attributes

6. PRESS: [Shift]+[Tab] to move to the options area
   PRESS: [↓] until the Read-only option is highlighted

7. To remove the attribute:
   PRESS: Space Bar

8. PRESS: [Enter]

9. Exit the DOS Shell.

....

Quick Reference   1. Select the file or files to modify.
Changing a File's   2. CHOOSE: File, Change Attributes
Attributes   3. Select the attributes to attach to the file or files.
                       4. PRESS: [Enter] or CLICK: OK

....

SUMMARY

This session introduced you to the DOS tools for managing files. The first half of the session concentrated on entering commands at the system prompt. To begin, you were shown how to select groups of files using the

DOS wildcard characters (* and ?). The primary file management commands, COPY, MOVE, REN, and DEL, were illustrated with hands-on examples. You also used the TYPE command to view the contents of a file and the ATTRIB command to modify the attributes of a file.

The last half of the session looked at the DOS Shell methods for performing file management commands. Beginning with commands for changing the color and screen mode, you also used the View command to customize the display of information in the DOS Shell. The majority of this section discussed the file management commands available under the File menu option: Copy, Move, Rename, Delete, View File Contents, and Change Attributes.

Many of the commands and procedures introduced in this session appear in the Command Summary (Table 2.5).

	Command	*Description*
Table 2.5		
Command Summary	COPY	Makes a duplicate of one or more files
	MOVE	Moves one or more files to a new drive or directory
	REN	Changes the name of one or more files
	DEL	Deletes one or more files
	UNDELETE	Restores one or more files
	TYPE	Views the contents of an ASCII text file
	ATTRIB	Views and changes the attributes of one or more files
DOS Shell Commands	Options, Colors	Changes the screen color of the DOS Shell
	Options, Display	Changes the screen mode of the DOS Shell
	View, *command*	Specifies the areas to view in the DOS Shell
	Options, File Display Options	Selects files to display in the File List area
	File, Copy	Copies the selected files from one location to another

	Command	Description
Table 2.5 (continued)	File, Move	Moves the selected files from one location to another
	File, Rename	Renames the selected files
	File, Delete	Deletes the selected files
	File, View File Contents	Views the contents of a file in text or hex format
	File, Change Attributes	Changes the attributes for the selected files

KEY TERMS

Add mode   The mode used for selecting multiple files in the File List area using the keyboard. The Add mode is invoked by pressing `Shift`+`F8`. With the Add mode turned on, you select and deselect files in the File List area by pressing the Space Bar.

ASCII   Acronym for American Standard Code for Information Interchange. An ASCII text file refers to an unformatted text file that can be viewed using DOS's TYPE command.

file attributes   Characteristics of a file that determine whether you can modify the file or display the file in a DIR listing. Use the ATTRIB command to view and change the file attributes, such as archive (a), read-only (r), hidden (h), and system (s).

file specification   Method of referring to a complete file name. A file specification consists of the drive letter, directory name, file name, and extension. Wildcard characters are used in a file specification to refer to a group of files.

Graphics mode   The DOS Shell screen mode that displays symbols and icons.

hex format   In the DOS Shell, the File, View File Contents command uses the hex view to display the contents of a formatted data file.

text format   In the DOS Shell, the File, View File Contents command uses the text view to display the contents of an ASCII text file.

Text mode   The DOS Shell screen mode that displays plain text characters, as opposed to symbols and icons.

wildcard characters   The asterisk (*) and question mark (?) are the DOS wildcard characters. The asterisk represents a group of characters, a file name, or an extension in a file specification. The question mark represents a single character in a file specification.

EXERCISES

SHORT ANSWER

1. What is the result of the following command: `dir /od /a-r /p`?
2. What does the asterisk represent in a file specification? the question mark? Give examples.
3. Name two methods for changing the name of a file.
4. Explain the limitations of the TYPE command.
5. What is the purpose of the read-only file attribute?
6. What is the purpose of the View command in the DOS Shell?
7. Explain the Add mode for selecting files using the keyboard.
8. Name two ways to delete a file after it has been selected in the File List area.
9. What are the two formats for viewing files using the File, View File Contents command?
10. What are the three levels of protection against accidentally deleting files? Which level offers the most security?

HANDS-ON

(*Note*: In the following exercises, you perform DOS commands using files located on the Advantage Diskette.)

1. The objective of this exercise is to practice some of the DOS file management commands that were entered from the command line in this session.
    a. Ensure that the A:\> system prompt is displayed.

   b. Perform a directory listing of all files that do not have an extension, sorted by file name:
   TYPE: `dir *. /on`
   PRESS: (Enter)

   c. Perform a directory listing of all the WK1 files, sorted by the creation date in descending order.

   d. Perform a directory listing that displays only the Q1, Q2, Q3, and Q4 files. Sort the listing by size.

   e. Create backup copies for all the Q?.WK1 files. Use the extension 123 for the duplicates.

   f. Rename all the files with a 123 extension to have a WBK extension (WBK stands for worksheet backup in this exercise).

   g. Delete the Q1.WBK file.

   h. Delete all the WBK files.

2. This exercise practices some of the file management commands that were executed from the DOS Shell in this session.

   a. Ensure that the A:\> system prompt is displayed.

   b. Load the DOS Shell.

   c. Customize the display to view a single Directory Tree and File List area.

   d. Select the File List area for drive A:.

   e. Limit the File List area to displaying only files that do not have extensions. Sort the list by file name.

   f. Limit the File List area to displaying only the WK1 files, sorted by the creation date in descending order.

   g. Using the keyboard, select the Q1, Q2, Q3, and Q4 files. Your screen should appear similar to Figure 2.14.

Figure 2.14

Selecting the Q1,
Q2, Q3, and Q4
files in the File
List area.

```
┌──────────────────────────────────────────────────────────────────┐
│                            MS-DOS Shell                            │
│  File  Options  View  Tree  Help                                   │
│ A:\                                                                │
│ ▣A    ▣B   ▢C   ▢H                                                 │
│ ┌────────────────────────┬──────────────────────────────────────┐ │
│ │     Directory Tree      │            A:\*.WK1                   │ │
│ │ ▭ A:\                  ↑│ ▤ EMPLOYEE.WK1    2,807  08-11-92  ↑ │ │
│ │                         │ ▤ SUMMARY .WK1    2,826  08-08-91    │ │
│ │                         │ ▤ SALES   .WK1    2,655  08-08-91    │ │
│ │                         │ ▤ Q4      .WK1    2,258  08-08-91    │ │
│ │                         │ ▤ Q3      .WK1    2,259  08-08-91    │ │
│ │                         │ ▤ Q2      .WK1    2,258  08-08-91    │ │
│ │                         │ ▤ Q1      .WK1    2,258  08-08-91    │ │
│ │                         │ ▤ INCOME  .WK1    3,718  08-08-91    │ │
│ │                         │ ▤ BUDGET  .WK1    2,771  08-08-91    │ │
│ │                         │ ▤ BILLS   .WK1    1,939  08-08-91    │ │
│ │                         │                            ▷         │ │
│ │                        ↓│                                   ↓ │ │
│ └────────────────────────┴──────────────────────────────────────┘ │
│ F10=Actions  Shift+F9=Command Prompt                        9:36p  │
└──────────────────────────────────────────────────────────────────┘
```

  h. Create backup copies for all the Q?.WK1 files. Use the extension
      123 for the duplicates.
  i. Rename all the files with a 123 extension to have a WBK extension.
  j. Delete the Q1.WBK file.
  k. Delete all the WBK files.
  l. View all files, sorted by name in ascending order.
  m. Exit the DOS Shell.

3. This exercise practices using the TYPE and ATTRIB commands from
    the command line and the DOS Shell.
    a. Ensure that the A:\> system prompt is displayed.
    b. In this exercise, imagine that an associate has saved a file called
        HARDWARE on the Advantage Diskette and has asked you to
        proofread it while she is out. To ensure that the file is on the
        diskette, you want to list all the files that are named HARDWARE:
        TYPE: dir hardware.*
        PRESS: (Enter)
        The directory listing presents three files: HARDWARE,
        HARDWARE.ASC, and HARDWARE.TXT.
    c. View the contents of the HARDWARE file using the TYPE
        command. Is this a formatted or unformatted data file?

d. View the contents of the HARDWARE.TXT file using the TYPE command. Is this a formatted or unformatted data file?

e. Because you do not want to accidentally modify your associate's file, attach a read-only attribute to the HARDWARE.TXT file.

f. Load the DOS Shell.

g. Using the DOS Shell, remove the read-only attribute that you just attached from the command line.

h. View the contents of the HARDWARE file using the DOS Shell. Is the file displayed in text or hex format?

i. View the contents of the HARDWARE.ASC file using the DOS Shell. Is the file displayed in text or hex format?

j. Exit the DOS Shell.

DOS 6:
WORKING WITH
DIRECTORIES

Some may argue that a well-organized hard disk is as important to productivity and performance as following sound time-management principles. You organize a hard disk by planning, creating, and implementing a logical directory structure. Like arranging folders in a filing cabinet or organizing your desk, you use directories to store related documents and bring some semblance of order to your everyday work.

PREVIEW

When you have completed this session, you will be able to:

Explain the importance of a directory structure.

•

Create, rename, and remove subdirectories.

•

Navigate and display the directory tree.

•

Copy and delete files in subdirectories.

•

Create a directory using the DOS Shell.

•

Copy files among directories using the DOS Shell.

•

Rename and remove a directory using the DOS Shell.

Why Is This Session Important?
The Directory Structure
Changing the DOS Prompt (PROMPT)
Using the Command Line
      Creating and Renaming a Directory (MD
         and MOVE)
      Changing to a Directory (CD)
      Copying and Moving Files
         to Subdirectories
      Removing a Directory (RD and
         DELTREE)
      Displaying the Directory Tree (TREE)
      Specifying a Search Path (PATH)
Using the DOS Shell
      Creating a Directory
      Changing to a Directory
      Copying and Moving Files
         to Subdirectories
      Removing a Directory
      Renaming a Directory
Summary
      Command Summary
Key Terms
Exercises
      Short Answer
      Hands-On

WHY IS THIS SESSION IMPORTANT?

This session introduces the DOS directory management commands. These commands focus on creating and working with directory structures on hard disks and floppy diskettes, rather than the individual files on those disks. In this session, you use the following commands from the command line to create, navigate, rename, and remove subdirectories:

CD	MOVE	RD
DELTREE	PATH	TREE
MD	PROMPT	

You also learn how to perform directory management using the DOS Shell.

Before proceeding, make sure the following are true:

1. You have turned on your computer system.
2. The C:\> system prompt is displayed on the screen.
3. Your Advantage Diskette is inserted into drive A:. You will work with files on the diskette that have been created for you.

THE DIRECTORY STRUCTURE

A directory structure provides the foundation for hard disk management. Program and data files are organized into separate subdirectories on a hard disk to facilitate storage, retrieval, and overall file management tasks. This session illustrates the advantages of a practical directory structure and lets you create, navigate, and manage a directory tree.

There are several approaches to designing a usable directory structure. The most important step consists of planning and estimating the number of application software programs and data files that you will store on the disk. Due to their large size and complexity, application software programs usually require a hard disk and a separate subdirectory for storage.

After purchasing a software program, you **install** or copy the program files from the enclosed floppy diskettes onto the hard disk. Most software programs provide detailed installation instructions and you simply respond to the prompts for inserting new diskettes. One of the first steps performed during installation is the creation of subdirectories for the main program files and the subsidiary help, tutorial, and example files. Although installation programs commonly create these subdirectories, you remain responsible for specifying and managing the location of your data files.

There are two main strategies for creating data file subdirectories:

1. *Keep program and data files together.*
   Programs sometimes assume that you want to keep your data files in the same directory as the program files, or in a subdirectory directly beneath the program directory. One disadvantage of this method is that your data files are spread throughout the directory structure. An example of this strategy follows:

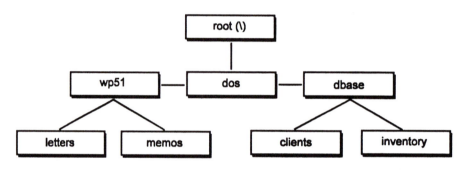

   This diagram shows the WordPerfect (wp51) and dBase (dbase) program directories with two subdirectories each for their data files. The letters and memos subdirectories contain the data for WordPerfect, and the clients and inventory subdirectories contain the data for dBase.

2. *Maintain two separate branches for program and data files.*
   To facilitate backup and search procedures, this strategy promotes a centralized data file area. Rather than storing data files in their respective program subdirectories, a separate **branch** is created in the directory structure. As explained later in this guide, this structure facilitates the process of backing up your hard disk. An example of this strategy follows:

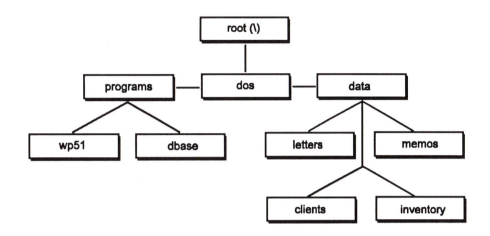

In this diagram, the WordPerfect and dBase programs appear in a subdirectory dedicated to storing program files. The four data file subdirectories (letters, memos, clients, and inventory) all appear immediately under the data subdirectory.

As with any important task, you need to plan the directory structure before sitting down at the computer. Sketch or draw your directory structure using an "organizational chart" format, similar to the diagrams appearing in this section. Your time is better spent planning than reconstructing a directory tree.

CHANGING THE DOS PROMPT (PROMPT)

The DOS system prompt displays information about your current drive and directory location, also called the **default** drive and directory. You can customize the system prompt using the PROMPT command. For most computers, this command appears in the AUTOEXEC.BAT file and is executed each time you boot the computer.

The syntax for the PROMPT command follows:

PROMPT [*text or codes*], or
PROMPT PG

The default prompt displays the drive letter and a greater-than sign (for example, C>). You use the PROMPT PG command to add the path name to the system prompt (for example, C:\DOS>). Although there are several options for customizing the system prompt, the PROMPT PG is the most common form of the command.

Perform the following steps.

1. Ensure that the Advantage Diskette is placed into drive A: and that the C:\> system prompt is displayed.

2. To display the default system prompt (the prompt that is displayed if no PROMPT command appears in the AUTOEXEC.BAT file):
   TYPE: `prompt`
   PRESS: [Enter]
   Notice that the default system prompt displays the drive letter (C), but not the root directory symbol (\).

3. To display the most widely accepted system prompt:
   TYPE: `prompt $p$g`
   On most computers, this version of the PROMPT command appears in the AUTOEXEC.BAT file.

....
Quick Reference   Command: PROMPT (internal)
PROMPT   Syntax: prompt pg
Command   Purpose: Changes the DOS system prompt for the command line
....

USING THE COMMAND LINE

As with file management, there are a limited number of DOS commands required to perform the majority of directory-related tasks. In this section, you create a subdirectory using the MD command, rename a directory using MOVE, navigate the directory tree with the CD command, and remove a directory using the RD and DELTREE commands. You are also introduced to the TREE command for displaying a pictorial view of the directory structure and the PATH command for telling DOS where to find program files.

CREATING AND RENAMING A DIRECTORY (MD AND MOVE)

When you prepare a new hard disk or diskette for storage, there are no subdirectories on the disk. However, every disk has a root or main directory. For hard disks, the root directory serves as the table of contents to the subdirectories on a disk. Because of the limited space on floppy diskettes, the root directory is primarily used for storage. The backslash character (\) symbolizes the root directory in DOS commands.

A directory structure is often called a directory tree because it branches out with each additional subdirectory. In this section, you will create the following directory tree on the Advantage Diskette:

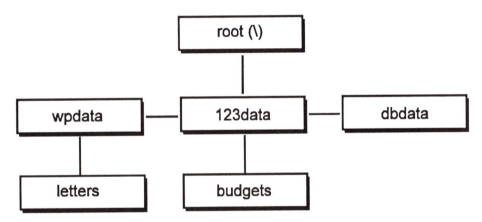

Each directory has a **path name** that tells DOS where the subdirectory is located in the directory tree. A full path name for a subdirectory always begins at the root directory (\). For example, the path name for WPDATA is \WPDATA. The backslash tells DOS to start at the top of the directory tree and then to move down one level to find the WPDATA subdirectory.

The path name for the LETTERS subdirectory is \WPDATA\LETTERS. The parts of this path name include:

1. first backslash (\)	tells DOS to start at the root, or the top of the directory tree
2. WPDATA	tells DOS to move down one level in the tree to the WPDATA subdirectory
3. second backslash (\)	separates one subdirectory's name from another

4. LETTERS   tells DOS to move down one more level in
                                    the directory tree to the LETTERS directory

The MD (MAKE DIRECTORY) command creates a subdirectory using
the following syntax:

MD *pathname*, or
MKDIR *pathname*

You can also rename a directory, whether or not it contains files, using the
MOVE command and the following syntax:

MOVE *oldname newname*

Perform the following steps to practice creating directories.

1. Ensure that the C:\> system prompt is displayed.

2. Move to drive A:.

3. Retrieve a directory listing of all files that have no extension:
    TYPE: dir *.
    PRESS: (Enter)

4. To create a directory for WordPerfect data files called WPDATA:
    TYPE: md \wpdata
    PRESS: (Enter)
    (*Note*: You do not have to use the full path name with the MD
    command. If you simply enter the subdirectory name—in this case,
    WPDATA rather than \WPDATA—the directory is still created.
    However, you should specify the full path name to prevent mistakes
    when you are first learning about subdirectories.)

5. To create a new directory for Lotus 1-2-3 data files:
    TYPE: md \123wks
    PRESS: (Enter)

6. Let's change the name of the 123WKS directory to 123DATA:
    TYPE: move \123wks \123data
    PRESS: (Enter)

7. To view the new subdirectories, perform another directory listing of all files that have no extension:

TYPE: dir *.

PRESS: [Enter]

Because the new subdirectories do not have extensions, they appear with the other files in the directory listing. Your screen should now appear similar to Figure 3.1.

Figure 3.1

Displaying subdirectories using the DIR command.

```
A:\>md \wpdata

A:\>md \123wks

A:\>move \123wks \123data
a:\123wks => a:\123data [ok]

A:\>dir *.

 Volume in drive A has no label
 Volume Serial Number is 1049-1ADD
 Directory of A:\

BUDGET                      897 08-31-92   3:48p
HARDWARE                  5,150 08-31-92   3:46p
NAMES                       966 09-01-92  10:07a
WPMICRO                   2,870 09-01-92   4:39p
WPSPELL                   4,447 08-08-91  12:00p
WPTEMP                      905 08-31-92   3:16p
WPDATA        <DIR>             03-21-94  10:01p
123DATA       <DIR>             03-21-94  10:01p
        8 file(s)          15,235 bytes
                          612,352 bytes free

A:\>
```

8. To create another subdirectory for storing dBASE data files:

TYPE: md \dbdata

PRESS: [Enter]

9. To create the LETTERS directory under the WPDATA subdirectory:

TYPE: md \wpdata\letters

PRESS: [Enter]

10. To create the BUDGETS directory under the 123DATA subdirectory:

TYPE: md \123data\budgets

PRESS: [Enter]

11. Let's use the MOVE command to rename the DBDATA directory as
    DB4DATA:
    TYPE: `move \dbdata \db4data`
    PRESS: Enter

12. To rename the WPDATA directory as WP6DATA:
    TYPE: `move \wpdata \wp6data`
    PRESS: Enter

13. To list the directories:
    TYPE: `dir *.`
    PRESS: Enter
    Notice that only the subdirectories existing in the root directory are
    displayed. The LETTERS and BUDGETS directories do not appear
    because they are on the second level of the directory tree.

14. To view the contents of the WP6DATA directory:
    TYPE: `dir \wp6data`
    PRESS: Enter
    Your screen should now appear similar to Figure 3.2.

Figure 3.2

Displaying the
contents of the
WP6DATA
subdirectory.

```
BUDGET                 897 08-31-92   3:48p
HARDWARE             5,150 08-31-92   3:46p
NAMES                  966 09-01-92  10:07a
WPMICRO              2,870 09-01-92   4:39p
WPSPELL              4,447 08-08-91  12:00p
WPTEMP                 905 08-31-92   3:16p
WP6DATA      <DIR>         03-21-94  10:01p
123DATA      <DIR>         03-21-94  10:01p
DB4DATA      <DIR>         03-21-94  10:03p
        9 file(s)        15,235 bytes
                        609,280 bytes free

A:\>dir \wp6data

 Volume in drive A has no label
 Volume Serial Number is 1049-1ADD
 Directory of A:\WP6DATA

.            <DIR>         03-21-94  10:01p
..           <DIR>         03-21-94  10:01p
LETTERS      <DIR>         03-21-94  10:04p
        3 file(s)             0 bytes
                        609,280 bytes free

A:\>
```

Although there are no files stored in the WP6DATA subdirectory, two
files appear in the directory listing with the LETTERS subdirectory.

DOS automatically places the single dot (. <DIR>) and double dot (.. <DIR>) directory entries in all subdirectories. The single dot entry represents the current directory and the double dot entry represents the preceding level in the directory tree, called the **parent directory**. Although the single dot entry serves little functional purpose, the double dot is used in conjunction with the CD command to move around a directory tree (discussed in the next section).

15. Clear the screen.

....
Quick Reference   Command: MD (internal)
MD Command   Syntax: md *pathname*
                     Purpose: Makes a new directory
....

CHANGING TO A DIRECTORY (CD)

At this point, you have an empty directory structure on the Advantage Diskette with files existing only in the root directory. This directory structure is similar to a filing cabinet with empty drawers or folders. To open one of the drawers in the cabinet, you use the CD or CHDIR command to change the current directory. The syntax for the CD (CHANGE DIRECTORY) command follows:

CD *pathname*, or
CHDIR *pathname*

Perform the following steps to practice moving among directories.

1. At the A:\> system prompt, enter the following command to move to the 123DATA subdirectory:
   TYPE: cd \123data
   PRESS: (Enter)
   Notice that the system prompt (A:\123DATA>) includes the current directory path name and drive letter. (*Note*: You do not have to use the full path name with the CD command in this instance. You could simply enter the subdirectory name, 123DATA rather than \123DATA. However, you should specify the full path name to prevent mistakes when you are first learning about subdirectories.)

2. Perform a directory listing:
   TYPE: `dir`
   PRESS: `Enter`
   You should see the BUDGETS directory appear in the listing with the single dot (. <DIR>) and double dot (.. <DIR>) entries.

3. To move to the DB4DATA subdirectory:
   TYPE: `cd \db4data`
   PRESS: `Enter`
   Notice that the system prompt changes to reflect the current directory.

4. To move to the LETTERS directory, you enter the full path name:
   TYPE: `cd \wp6data\letters`
   PRESS: `Enter`

5. To move to the WP6DATA subdirectory, in the preceding level of the directory tree, you can use a shortcut:
   TYPE: `cd..`
   PRESS: `Enter`
   Notice that the command takes you to the parent directory, WP6DATA.

6. To move to the top of the directory tree, or the root directory:
   TYPE: `cd \`
   PRESS: `Enter`

In the next section, you copy files from the root directory of the Advantage Diskette into the various subdirectories on the disk.

....
Quick Reference   Command: CD (internal)
CD Command   Syntax: cd *pathname*
                         Purpose: Changes to another directory
....

COPYING AND MOVING FILES TO SUBDIRECTORIES

To copy and move files among directories, you use the COPY and MOVE commands introduced in Session 2. To refresh your memory, the syntax for both commands follows:

COPY *source destination*
MOVE *source destination*

In specifying the source and destination parameters, you must include the path name in the file specification. A complete file name consists of the drive letter, path name, file name, and extension. For example, review the complete file name listed below:

A:\123DATA\BUDGETS\BUD1994.WK1

The parts of this file name include:

1. A: tells DOS that the file is located in drive A:

2. \123DATA\BUDGETS   tells DOS the directory path name where the file is stored

3. Backslash (\)   separates the subdirectory name from the file name

4. BUD1994   the file name

5. WK1   the file extension

It is very important that you do not enter any spaces between the drive letter, directory path name, and the file name. There are only two spaces in the COPY or MOVE command—one space between the command and the source, and another space between the source and the destination.

When you are performing file management commands on the current disk drive, you can leave off the drive letter in the file specification. DOS assumes that the current disk is the default drive when no letter is specified in the command.

Perform the following steps.

1. Ensure that the A:\> system prompt is displayed.

2. To copy the EXAMPLE.TXT file into the WP6DATA directory:
   TYPE: copy example.txt \wp6data
   PRESS: [Enter]
   Notice that you do not need to enter the drive letter or path name for the source because it exists in the current directory.

3. To confirm that the copy procedure worked:
   TYPE: `dir \wp6data`
   PRESS: (Enter)
   The EXAMPLE.TXT file appears in the listing.

4. To copy all the WK1 files to the BUDGETS directory:
   TYPE: `copy *.wk1 \123data\budgets`
   PRESS: (Enter)

5. To move the EXAMPLE.TXT file from the WP6DATA subdirectory to the LETTERS directory:
   TYPE: `move \wp6data\example.txt \wp6data\letters`
   PRESS: (Enter)

6. To move the Q1.WK1, Q2.WK1, Q3.WK1, and Q4.WK1 files from the BUDGETS subdirectory to the WP6DATA directory:
   TYPE: `move \123data\budgets\q?.wk1 \wp6data`
   PRESS: (Enter)

7. Clear the screen.

REMOVING A DIRECTORY (RD AND DELTREE)

When you are finished working with a subdirectory, you remove it using either the RD command or the DELTREE command. If you use the RD (REMOVE DIRECTORY) command, there are two conditions to meet before DOS allows you to remove a directory:

1. *The directory must be empty.*
   There cannot be any files or subdirectories in the directory that you want to remove. Therefore, the first step in removing a directory with the RD command is to delete the existing files and subdirectories.

2. *You cannot be in the directory that you want to remove.*
   You cannot remove the current directory. To remove a directory, move to its parent directory or to the root directory before issuing the RD command. (*Note*: You cannot remove the root directory.)

With large directory structures, removing a directory can be quite tedious if you have to first delete the files in each of its subdirectories (also called pruning the directory tree). To facilitate this process, DOS 6 introduces a new command called DELTREE, which allows you to wipe out multiple directories (and their subdirectories and files) with a single command.

Obviously, DELTREE is a dangerous command and should only be used with due care.

The syntax for the RD and DELTREE commands follows:

RD *pathname*, or
RMDIR *pathname*

DELTREE *pathname [pathname1] [...]*

Perform the following steps to practice removing directories.

1. Ensure that the A:\> system prompt is displayed.

2. This step attempts to remove the \123DATA\BUDGETS directory using the RD command. Because there are files in this subdirectory, the first condition for removing a directory using RD is not met. This step illustrates DOS's reaction when you attempt to use the RD command to remove a directory that is not empty:
   TYPE: `rd \123data\budgets`
   PRESS: (Enter)
   The message "Invalid path, not directory, or directory not empty" appears and you are returned to the system prompt.

3. To remove the \123DATA\BUDGETS directory using the RD command, you must first remove the files in the subdirectory:
   TYPE: `del \123data\budgets\*.*`
   PRESS: (Enter)
   (*Note*: The file specification *.* stands for all files. You can also delete a directory of files using only the directory name in the DEL command. For example, the command `del \123data\budgets` produces the same results as the above command.)

4. When asked if you are sure that you want to delete all the files, answer yes to the prompt:
   TYPE: `y`
   PRESS: (Enter)

5. TYPE: `dir \123data\budgets`
   PRESS: (Enter)
   You should only see the single dot and double dot entries in the file listing. For the purposes of the RD command, this directory is now

empty and it can be removed. (*Note*: You cannot remove the single dot and double dot entries from a subdirectory.)

6. To remove the directory:
   TYPE: `rd \123data\budgets`
   PRESS: (Enter)

7. To make sure that you removed the BUDGETS directory, perform a listing of the 123DATA directory:
   TYPE: `dir \123data`
   PRESS: (Enter)
   You should not see the BUDGETS subdirectory in the directory listing.

8. Let's create some additional directories on the Advantage Diskette:
   TYPE: `md \xl5data`
   PRESS: (Enter)
   TYPE: `md \xl5data\graphs`
   PRESS: (Enter)
   TYPE: `md \xl5data\macros`
   PRESS: (Enter)
   TYPE: `md \qprodata`
   PRESS: (Enter)

9. To demonstrate how easy it is to use the DELTREE command to remove subdirectories:
   TYPE: `deltree \xl5data \qprodata`
   PRESS: (Enter)
   TYPE: `y` (to confirm the deletion of XL5DATA and its subdirectories)
   PRESS: (Enter)
   TYPE: `y` (to confirm the deletion of QPRODATA)
   PRESS: (Enter)
   All the subdirectories that you created in the previous step are removed with this single command.

10. Clear the screen.

Quick Reference	Command:	RD (internal) and DELTREE (external)
RD and DELTREE Commands	Syntax:	rd *pathname*, and deltree *pathname [pathname1] [pathname 2]*
	Purpose:	Removes a directory

DISPLAYING THE DIRECTORY TREE (TREE)

Many computer users become overzealous when it comes to organizing files into subdirectories. There are decreasing returns as you add more subdirectories and levels to your directory tree. Finding a file in a massive directory structure is similar to finding your way through a maze. Fortunately, DOS provides the TREE command for displaying a graphical view of a directory structure.

The syntax for the TREE command follows:

TREE *drive:* [/A] [/F]

The /A switch is optional and displays the directory tree using ASCII text characters rather than graphic characters. The ASCII characters enable you to print the directory tree using the redirection symbol discussed later in this guide. The /F switch displays the file names along with each branch of the directory tree.

Perform the following steps.

1. Ensure that the A:\> system prompt is displayed.

2. To display an ASCII picture of the directory structure:
    TYPE: `tree a: /a`
    PRESS: (Enter)

3. To display a graphical picture of the directory structure with files:
    TYPE: `tree a:`
    PRESS: (Enter)
    Your screen should now appear similar to Figure 3.3.

Figure 3.3

The results of the
TREE command
for drive A:.

```
A:\>tree a: /a
Directory PATH listing
Volume Serial Number is 1049-1ADD
A:.
+---WP6DATA
|   \---LETTERS
+---123DATA
\---DB4DATA

A:\>tree a:
Directory PATH listing
Volume Serial Number is 1049-1ADD
A:.
├───WP6DATA
│   └───LETTERS
├───123DATA
└───DB4DATA

A:\>
```

Quick Reference   Command: TREE (external)
TREE Command   Syntax: tree [*drive:*] [/a] [/f]
                        Purpose: Displays a graphical view of a directory structure

---

SPECIFYING A SEARCH PATH (PATH)

The PATH command enables you to execute program files stored on a
different disk or in a different subdirectory. As a reminder, program files
are files with COM (Command), EXE (Executable), and BAT (Batch)
extensions. The PATH command sets a **search path** for program files in
alternative locations on a computer. Without a path, DOS only looks in the
current or default directory for program files.

To use the DOS external commands from anywhere in the directory tree,
you must specify the DOS directory in the path. When you enter a
command to execute a program, DOS always looks in the current directory
first for the program file. If the program file is not found, DOS searches the
directories that are specified in the path. If the program file is still not
located, the error message "Bad command or file name" is displayed. The
PATH command typically appears in the AUTOEXEC.BAT file so that it
executes each time the computer is booted.

The syntax for the PATH command follows:

PATH *pathname1*[;*pathname2*;...]

Perform the following steps.

1. Ensure that the A:\> system prompt is displayed.

2. To show the current search path:
    TYPE: path
    PRESS: [Enter]

    CAUTION: The next command changes the path. If you enter the PATH command and receive a "No path" message, then proceed to the next step. However, if several directory names appear next to the "PATH=" statement, you should not change the path setting without the permission of your instructor.

3. If you received the "No path" message in the previous step, specify a path that tells DOS to search the root directory and the DOS directory of drive C: each time a command is issued:
    TYPE: path c:\;c:\dos
    PRESS: [Enter]
    With the path set for the DOS directory, you no longer have to worry about receiving an error message when issuing external DOS commands. Remember that external DOS command files are commonly kept in the DOS subdirectory.

    CAUTION: It is possible that the external DOS program files are stored in a subdirectory other than C:\DOS (perhaps C:\DOS6.) In this case, substitute the appropriate subdirectory name into the path statement for the C:\DOS subdirectory. You may need to get this information from your instructor.

4. Clear the screen.

....

Quick Reference   Command: PATH (internal)
PATH Command   Syntax: path *pathname1* [;*pathname2*;...]
                          Purpose: Displays or sets the search path for program files

....

USING THE DOS SHELL

The DOS Shell eases the task of directory management. To change the current directory, you simply highlight the desired folder in the Directory Tree area. To create, rename, and remove subdirectories, you choose commands from the Menu bar. In this section, you'll explore these commands and practice copying files among directories.

For file management, you select the File List area before issuing a file management command. For disk management, you select the Directory Tree area. The Directory Tree area displays the directory structure for the current disk drive, with folders representing the individual subdirectories.

CREATING A DIRECTORY

You create a directory using the File, Create Directory command from the Menu bar. Before you issue the command, however, you must select the desired parent directory in the Directory Tree area. On a new or blank disk, the parent directory is always the root directory.

Let's practice creating subdirectories on the Advantage Diskette.

1. Ensure that the A:\> system prompt is displayed.

2. Load the DOS Shell program:
   TYPE: dosshell
   PRESS: Enter

3. Make sure that you have selected the following options:
   CHOOSE: View, Single File List
   CHOOSE: Options, File Display Options
   TYPE: *.*
   SELECT: Name in the Sort by group
   SELECT: Ascending order
   PRESS: Enter
   To sort the files in ascending order requires that no × appear in the Descending order check box.

4. SELECT: Directory Tree area

5. To create a new directory, you select the parent directory and then issue the File, Create Directory command. Place a new subdirectory called BATCH under the root directory:

SELECT: A:\ (not the folder, but the text) in the Directory Tree area

CHOOSE: File, Create Directory

A dialog box appears for you to type the name of the new directory (Figure 3.4).

Figure 3.4

The File, Create Directory dialog box.

```
                          MS-DOS Shell
 File  Options  View  Tree  Help
A:\
 ═A    ═B   ═C   ═H

        Directory Tree                         A:\*.*
    A:\                          ↑  ▒ BILLS    .WK1    1,939  08-08-91  ↑
      123DA┌──────────── Create Directory ──────────────┐7  08-31-92
      DB4DA│                                             │1  08-08-91
      WP6DA│                                             │5  08-31-92
           │  Parent name: A:\                           │7  08-11-92
           │                                             │0  10-26-92
           │  New directory name. .  ┌─────────┐         │4  11-09-92
           │                         └─────────┘         │0  08-31-92
           │                                             │0  10-29-92
           │                                             │0  10-29-92
           │                                             │8  08-08-91
           │                                             │6  09-01-92
           │  ( OK )      ( Cancel )      ( Help )        │8  08-08-91
           │                                             │8  08-08-91
           └─────────────────────────────────────────────┘9  08-08-91
                          ▒ Q4        .WK1    2,258  08-08-91
                          ▒ SALES     .MAR      779  08-31-92
                          ▒ SALES     .WK1    2,655  08-08-91
                          ▒ SEMINAR   .LET      997  09-17-92
                          ▒ SOFTWARE.1        3,337  08-31-92
                          ▒ SOFTWARE.4        3,337  09-01-92
                          ▒ STATS     .XLS    2,246  08-31-92
                       ↓  ▒ SUMMARY   .WK1    2,826  08-08-91  ↓
 F10=Actions   Shift+F9=Command Prompt                     10:21p
```

6. To create the BATCH subdirectory:

TYPE: batch

PRESS: (Enter)

Notice that a new branch is created for the BATCH subdirectory in the directory tree.

7. To create a new directory called PROJECTS under the 123DATA directory:

SELECT: 123DATA in the Directory Tree area

CHOOSE: File, Create Directory

8. Make sure the parent name in the dialog box is A:\123DATA and then enter the name of the new directory:
    TYPE: `projects`
    PRESS: (Enter)
    Notice that the new PROJECTS directory is attached to its parent directory, 123DATA.

9. SELECT: A:\ in the Directory Tree area

Quick Reference
Creating a New
Subdirectory

1. Select the parent directory in the Directory Tree area.
2. CHOOSE: File, Create Directory
3. Type the name of the new subdirectory.
4. PRESS: (Enter) or CLICK: OK

CHANGING TO A DIRECTORY

To move to a different directory in the Directory Tree area, you use the cursor-movement keys or the mouse to highlight the desired folder. When you select a folder, the files within the directory are displayed in the File List area. However, not all subdirectories are always displayed in the Directory Tree area.

The Directory Tree area is similar to an outline, where you expand or collapse topics to view more or less detail. If a directory contains subdirectories that are not currently displayed in the tree diagram, a plus sign (+) appears in the parent directory folder. A minus sign (–) in a parent directory folder tells you that all subdirectories are displayed.

You expand and collapse branches in the directory tree using the keyboard, mouse, or Tree option on the menu. The Tree option contains four commands for manipulating the tree diagram, as described in Table 3.1 with menu and shortcut key methods.

Table 3.1	*Command*	*Keyboard Shortcut*	*Description*
T̲ree Commands	E̲xpand One Level	+	Displays one additional level in the directory tree for the highlighted branch
	Expand B̲ranch	*	Displays all subdirectory levels under the currently selected branch
	Expand A̲ll	Ctrl +*	Displays all subdirectory levels on the drive
	C̲ollapse Branch	-	Collapses all subdirectory levels for a given branch

To practice expanding and collapsing the directory tree diagram, perform the following steps.

1. SELECT: A:\ in the Directory Tree area
   Notice that the folder has a minus sign (–).

2. To collapse the branch using the keyboard, press the minus sign:
   TYPE: –
   Notice that the A:\ folder now has a plus sign (+), indicating that it contains subdirectories that are not currently displayed.

3. To expand the branch using the keyboard, press the plus sign:
   PRESS: +

4. To expand the WP6DATA branch using the mouse, click on the plus sign in the WP6DATA folder:
   CLICK: +

5. To collapse the WP6DATA branch using the mouse, click on the minus sign in the folder:
   CLICK: –

6. To collapse the entire directory diagram using the T̲ree menu option:
   SELECT: A:\ (click on the text "A:\", to the right of the folder icon)
   CHOOSE: T̲ree, C̲ollapse Branch

7. To expand the entire directory tree diagram using the menu:
    CHOOSE: Tree, Expand All
    Your screen should now appear similar to Figure 3.5.

Figure 3.5

The Directory
Tree area after
choosing the
Tree, Expand All
command.

```
                            MS-DOS Shell
   File  Options  View  Tree  Help
  A:\
  [=]A   [=]B  [ ]C  [ ]H

         Directory Tree                      A:\*.*
  [-] A:\                           ↑  [▒] BILLS    .WK1    1,939  08-08-91 ↑
     └[ ] 123DATA                      [▒] BUDGET             897  08-31-92
        └[ ] PROJECTS                  [▒] BUDGET   .WK1    2,771  08-08-91
     └[ ] BATCH                        [▒] CASH     .XLS    6,265  08-31-92
     └[ ] DB4DATA                      [▒] EMPLOYEE .WK1    2,807  08-11-92
     └[ ] WP6DATA                      [▒] EXAMPLE  .TXT      500  10-26-92
        └[ ] LETTERS                   [▒] EXPENSES .DBF    8,994  11-09-92
                                       [▒] HARDWARE         5,150  08-31-92
                                       [▒] HARDWARE .ASC    1,440  10-29-92
                                       [▒] HARDWARE .TXT    1,440  10-29-92
                                       [▒] INCOME   .WK1    3,718  08-08-91
                                       [▒] NAMES             966  09-01-92
                                       [▒] Q1       .WK1    2,258  08-08-91
                                       [▒] Q2       .WK1    2,258  08-08-91
                                       [▒] Q3       .WK1    2,259  08-08-91
                                       [▒] Q4       .WK1    2,258  08-08-91
                                       [▒] SALES    .MAR      779  08-31-92
                                       [▒] SALES    .WK1    2,655  08-08-91
                                       [▒] SEMINAR  .LET      997  09-17-92
                                       [▒] SOFTWARE .1      3,337  08-31-92
                                       [▒] SOFTWARE .4      3,337  09-01-92
                                       [▒] STATS    .XLS    2,246  08-31-92
                                    ↓  [▒] SUMMARY  .WK1    2,826  08-08-91 ↓
   F10=Actions   Shift+F9=Command Prompt                           10:26p
```

Quick Reference   CHOOSE: Tree, *command*, where *command* is one of the following:
Expanding and   • Expand One Level   Display one additional subdirectory level
Collapsing the   • Expand Branch   Display all subdirectory levels for a branch
Directory Tree Area   • Expand All   Display all subdirectory levels on a drive
                         • Collapse Branch   Collapse subdirectory levels for a branch

---

COPYING AND MOVING FILES TO SUBDIRECTORIES

Copying and moving files among subdirectories is identical to copying and
moving files between drives. You select the files that you want to
manipulate and then you issue the File, Copy or File, Move command. In
the dialog box, you enter the name of the target directory for the files (for
example, \BATCH). You can also use the drag and drop method to copy
files between disk drives or between subdirectory folders.

Perform the following steps.

1. To copy files from one directory into another, you must first select the source folder in the Directory Tree area:
   SELECT: A:\
   The files for the root directory of drive A: appear in the File List area.

2. SELECT: EXAMPLE.TXT file from the File List area

3. CHOOSE: File, Copy

4. To copy the EXAMPLE.TXT file to the BATCH subdirectory, enter the destination in the Copy dialog box:
   TYPE: \batch
   PRESS: Enter

5. To verify that the copy procedure worked:
   CLICK: BATCH in the Directory Tree area
   The EXAMPLE.TXT file appears in the File List area.

6. To move the files from the WP6DATA directory to the DB4DATA directory, first select the files:
   CLICK: WP6DATA in the Directory Tree area
   PRESS: Tab to move to the File List area
   PRESS: Ctrl+/ to select all the files

7. Position the mouse over the highlighted files in the File List area.

8. CLICK: left mouse button and hold down
   DRAG: mouse pointer over DB4DATA in the Directory Tree area

9. When the mouse pointer is positioned directly on top of DB4DATA, release the left mouse button. A dialog box appears, confirming the move operation (Figure 3.6).

Figure 3.6

Moving files using
the drag and drop
method.

```
┌──────────────────────────────────────────────────────────────┐
│                          MS-DOS Shell                          │
│   File  Options  View  Tree  Help                              │
│  A:\WP6DATA                                                    │
│  [▣]A   [▣]B   [□]C   [□]H                                      │
│ ┌──────────────────────┐            A:\WP6DATA\*.*             │
│ │   Directory Tree     │  ↑ [▣] Q1      .WK1     2,258  08-08-91│↑
│ │ ⊟ A:\           ┌──────────────────────────┐  2,258  08-08-91│
│ │  ├─ 123DATA     │   Confirm Mouse Operation │  2,259  08-08-91│
│ │  │  └─ PROJECT  │                           │  2,258  08-08-91│
│ │  ├─ BATCH       │  Are you sure you want to move              │
│ │  ├─ DB4DATA     │  the selected files to                      │
│ │  ├─ WP6DATA     │  A:\DB4DATA?                                │
│ │  │  └─ LETTERS  │                           │                 │
│ │                 │    ( Yes )     (  No  )   │                 │
│ │                 └──────────────────────────┘                 │
│ │                                                              │
│ │                                            ↓               ↓ │
│  Move files to DB4DATA                                  10:29p  │
└──────────────────────────────────────────────────────────────┘
```

10. To complete the move operation:
     PRESS: [Enter] or CLICK: Yes

REMOVING A DIRECTORY

You remove a subdirectory using the File, Delete command from the Menu
bar or the [Delete] key. Make sure that you position the Selection cursor
on the desired subdirectory folder before issuing either command. As in the
command line procedure for using the RD command, you must first delete
the files and subdirectories in the directory you want removed.

Perform the following steps.

1. To remove the PROJECTS directory under the 123DATA directory:
    SELECT: PROJECTS in the Directory Tree area

2. CHOOSE: File, Delete
    PRESS: [Enter] or CLICK: Yes

3. To remove the BATCH directory:
    SELECT: BATCH in the Directory Tree area
    SELECT: EXAMPLE.TXT in the File List area

4. To delete the EXAMPLE.TXT file:
   PRESS: [Delete]
   PRESS: [Enter] or CLICK: Yes

5. To delete the BATCH Directory:
   PRESS: [Delete]
   PRESS: [Enter] or CLICK: Yes

....

Quick Reference
Removing a
Subdirectory

1. Select the subdirectory to remove in the Directory Tree area.
2. Delete the files appearing in the File List area.
3. CHOOSE: File, Delete or PRESS: [Delete]
4. PRESS: [Enter] or CLICK: Yes

....

RENAMING A DIRECTORY

The File, Rename command allows you to rename both files and subdirectories. As with most commands in the DOS Shell, you must select the directory that you want renamed before issuing the command.

Perform the following steps.

1. SELECT: LETTERS in the Directory Tree area

2. To rename the LETTERS directory to MEMOS:
   CHOOSE: File, Rename
   A dialog box appears for you to enter the new directory name.

3. TYPE: memos
   PRESS: [Enter]
   Notice that the tree diagram immediately changes to reflect the new directory name.

4. Exit the DOS Shell.

....

Quick Reference
Renaming a
Subdirectory

1. Select the subdirectory to rename in the Directory Tree area.
2. CHOOSE: File, Rename
3. Type the new directory name in the dialog box.
4. PRESS: [Enter] or CLICK: OK

....

SUMMARY

This session introduced you to the DOS directory management commands. You created a directory structure, moved through the directory tree, copied and moved files from one directory to another, and removed subdirectories. To begin the session, you customized the system prompt at the command line to provide disk, path, and system information. You also set a search path so that DOS could find program files on other disks and in other directories.

Directory management using the DOS Shell consumed the latter half of the session. You performed directory tasks using commands in the Menu bar, including creating, removing, and renaming subdirectories. Many of the commands and procedures introduced in this session appear in Table 3.2.

Table 3.2	*Command*	*Description*
Command Summary	PROMPT	Changes the DOS system prompt for the command line
	MD or MKDIR	Makes a new directory
	MOVE	Moves files and renames directories
	CD or CHDIR	Displays or changes to a directory
	RD or RMDIR	Removes a directory
	DELTREE	Removes a directory or multiple directories, including all subdirectories and files in the directory branch
	TREE	Displays a graphical view of a directory structure
	PATH	Displays or sets the search path for program files
DOS Shell Commands	File, Create Directory	Creates a new directory
	Tree, *command*	Expands and collapses the Directory Tree area
	File, Delete	Removes a directory
	File, Rename	Renames a directory

KEY TERMS

branch   In a directory structure, a branch refers to a level in the directory tree. For example, subdirectories branch out from the root directory to form the first level in the directory tree.

default   Any value that DOS assumes is true unless specifically told otherwise. The current disk drive and directory are the default drive and directory that are automatically affected by commands unless the user specifies otherwise.

install   The process of copying program files from original master diskette(s) to your hard disk or floppy diskette(s). Often, application software programs are shipped in a compressed format on the master diskettes and then decompressed onto the hard disk.

parent directory   In a directory structure, *parent directory* refers to the directory in the immediately preceding level of the directory tree. For example, the root directory is the parent directory for the first level of subdirectories. The first level subdirectories are the parents for the second level subdirectories.

path name   In a directory structure, *path name* refers to the complete name of a subdirectory, beginning at the root directory. For example, the path name \WINDOWS\CLIPART refers to the CLIPART directory on the second level of the directory tree. WINDOWS is the parent directory for CLIPART and the root directory (\) is the parent directory for WINDOWS.

search path   The names of disk drives and subdirectories to search for program files, including batch files (*.BAT), command files (*.COM), and executable files (*.EXE). Unless a path is set using the PATH command, DOS only looks in the default directory for program files.

EXERCISES

SHORT ANSWER

1. Given the path name \TOOLS\DISK\NORTON, what is the parent directory for the DISK subdirectory? If this complete path appeared on drive D: and a file called NU.COM appeared in the NORTON subdirectory, what is the complete name of the NU.COM file?
2. What is the command to display the drive letter and path name in the system prompt?
3. What is the command to return to the root directory from anywhere in the directory tree?
4. What is the quickest way to move from the current directory to its parent directory?
5. What two conditions must be met before DOS allows you to remove a subdirectory using the RD command?
6. What does a plus sign represent on a folder icon in the Directory Tree area? a minus sign?
7. What command do you choose from the Menu bar to view all the branches in the Directory Tree area?
8. Once a directory is highlighted in the Directory Tree area, how do you select all the files in the File List area?
9. What assumptions are made by DOS when you use the drag and drop method to drag files between drives? between directories on the same drive?
10. What command do you use to rename a directory at the command line?

HANDS-ON

(Note: In the following exercises, you perform DOS commands using files located on the Advantage Diskette.)

1. The objective of this exercise is to create the directory structure that appears in Figure 3.7. Given that you performed the hands-on examples in this session, several of the desired directories already exist on the Advantage Diskette.

Figure 3.7

An example
directory structure.

```
A:\>tree
Directory PATH listing
Volume Serial Number is 1049-1ADD
A:.
├──WP6DATA
│    ├──MEMOS
│    ├──LETTERS
│    │    ├──HOME
│    │    └──WORK
│    └──AGENDAS
├──123DATA
│    ├──1993
│    ├──1994
│    └──1995
├──DB4DATA
│    ├──PRODUCTS
│    ├──INVENTRY
│    ├──EMPLOYEE
│    └──CONTACTS
└──PROGRAMS
     ├──123R24
     ├──DBASE
     └──WP

A:\>
```

    a. Ensure that the A:\> system prompt is displayed.

    b. From the command line, create the PROGRAMS subdirectory and the three additional directories that branch out from PROGRAMS.

    c. From the command line, create three subdirectories for each year under the 123DATA directory.

    d. Load the DOS Shell.

    e. Create the four subdirectories appearing under the DB4DATA directory.

    f. Create the additional branches for the WP6DATA directory. Notice that the HOME and WORK directories appear on the third level of the directory tree, with the LETTERS directory as the parent.

    g. Exit the DOS Shell.

    h. Ensure that the printer is turned on and has sufficient paper. To send the output from the TREE command to the printer:
PRESS: [Ctrl]+[PrtScr]
TYPE: tree /a
PRESS: [Enter]
PRESS: [Ctrl]+[PrtScr]

2. This exercise practices copying files among directories using the command line and the DOS Shell. You must complete Exercise 1 to successfully complete this exercise.

    a. Ensure that the A:\> system prompt is displayed.

b. From the command line, copy the WK1 files in the root directory to the \123DATA\1993 subdirectory.

c. From the command line, copy the files that have no extension in the root directory to the HOME directory.

d. From the command line, copy the LET files in the root directory to the WORK directory.

e. Load the DOS Shell.

f. Expand the Directory Tree to view all the branches.

g. Move the files appearing in the DB4DATA directory to the AGENDAS directory using the commands in the Menu bar.

h. Move the files appearing in the 1993 directory to the 1994 directory using the drag and drop method.

i. Rename the INVENTRY directory as STOCK.

j. Exit the DOS Shell.

3. This exercise practices pruning a directory tree by removing unnecessary subdirectories.

a. Ensure that the A:\> system prompt is displayed.

b. From the command line, remove all the subdirectories appearing beneath the DB4DATA directory using the RD command.

c. From the command line, remove all the subdirectories appearing beneath the WP6DATA directory using the DELTREE command. (*Hint*: Do not remove the WP6DATA directory.)

d. Load the DOS Shell.

e. Remove all the subdirectories appearing beneath the 123DATA.

f. Exit the DOS Shell.

g. Send the output from the TREE command to the printer:
PRESS: Ctrl+PrtScr
TYPE: tree /a
PRESS: Enter
PRESS: Ctrl+PrtScr
The printed output should appear similar to Figure 3.8.

Figure 3.8

An example
directory structure.

```
A:\>tree /a
Directory PATH listing
Volume Serial Number is 1049-1ADD
A:.
+---WP6DATA
+---123DATA
+---DB4DATA
\---PROGRAMS
    +---123R24
    +---DBASE
    \---WP

A:\>
```

DOS 6:
MANAGING YOUR DISKS

Preventive maintenance keeps your body healthy, your car moving, and your computer running. But in spite of good care, problems still occur. Over time most hard disks will fail due to excessive use, power surges, or physical punishment. Fortunately, DOS provides several disk management commands to prolong the life of your hard disk and to minimize your losses if your hard disk fails.

PREVIEW

When you have completed this session, you will be able to:

Explain the basics of disk storage.

•

Format a new or an existing diskette.

•

Unformat an accidentally formatted disk.

•

Create, modify, and delete a disk's volume label.

•

Check the reliability of a disk.

•

Defragment the files on a disk.

•

Duplicate a floppy diskette.

•

Back up and restore your data files.

•

Perform disk management commands using the DOS Shell.

Why Is This Session Important?
Disk Storage Fundamentals
      Bits and Bytes
      Dividing a Disk
      Doubling a Disk's Capacity
Preventive Maintenance
      Protecting Your Computer
      Defragmenting a Disk (DEFRAG)
Using the Command Line
      Preparing a New Disk (FORMAT)
      Unformatting a Disk (UNFORMAT)
      Naming a Disk (VOL and LABEL)
      Checking the Reliability of a Disk (CHKDSK
          and SCANDISK)
      Copying an Entire Diskette (DISKCOPY)
      Backing Up and Restoring Your Data Files
          (MSBACKUP)
Using the DOS Shell
      Copying an Entire Diskette
      Formatting a Disk
Summary
      Command Summary
Key Terms
Exercises
      Short Answer
      Hands-On

WHY IS THIS SESSION IMPORTANT?

This session introduces the basics of data storage and retrieval for hard disks and floppy diskettes. You also explore the disk management commands provided by DOS for preventive maintenance, recovery, and other disk-related procedures. By the end of this session, you'll know how to use the following disk management commands:

CHKDSK   FORMAT   UNFORMAT
DEFRAG   LABEL   VOL
DISKCOPY   MSBACKUP
DBLSPACE   SCANDISK

If used incorrectly, some commands introduced in this session can adversely affect your disks. Rather than asking you to perform these particular commands, we illustrate their use with examples. *Read the instructions in this session carefully! If you are unsure about which steps to perform, ask your instructor.*

Before proceeding, make sure the following are true:

1. You have turned on your computer system.
2. The C:\> system prompt is displayed on the screen.
3. Your Advantage Diskette is inserted into drive A:. You will work with files on the diskette that have been created for you.

DISK STORAGE FUNDAMENTALS

On a computer, you perform your work in the random access memory (RAM). The advantage of working in memory is that data is transferred between RAM and the CPU very quickly. However, RAM is volatile and its contents are discarded when you perform a warm boot or turn off the computer's power. Therefore, you must save your work to the hard disk or a floppy diskette for permanent storage.

Data is stored on a disk using magnetic particles that coat the disk's surface. The **read/write heads** of a disk drive retrieve and write data by manipulating these magnetic particles. Similarly to the way a record needle picks up music from an album, the read/write heads lift data from a spinning disk. In floppy diskette drives, the read/write heads rest directly on the surface of the diskette, limiting the rotation speed to approximately 360 revolutions per minute (RPM). Hard disk drives are typically ten times faster than floppy diskette drives because the heads float on a layer of air over the disk surface. As a result, you can access data from hard disk drives much faster than from floppy diskette drives.

BITS AND BYTES

A **byte** is the basic measurement unit for computer storage. One byte is the amount of space required to store a single character of text. Each character is coded by a unique sequence of 8 **bits**, the binary digits 1 and 0 that are machine language.

A kilobyte (KB) is approximately one thousand bytes (1,024 bytes), or half a page of text. A megabyte (MB) is slightly greater than one million bytes (1,048,576 bytes), and a gigabyte (GB) is about one billion bytes (1,073,741,824 bytes).

The most common storage capacities for floppy diskettes are 360 KB, 720 KB, 1.2 MB, 1.44 MB, and 2.88 MB. Hard disk drives are available in a variety of capacities, commonly ranging from 80 MB to 340 MB.

DIVIDING A DISK

When you prepare a disk for storage using the FORMAT command, DOS divides the disk into tracks, cylinders, and sectors. **Tracks** are concentric rings on the disk's surface where DOS stores data. Most disks are double-sided, and therefore there are two sets of read/write heads—one on each side. A pair of tracks that occupy the same position on opposite sides of a disk is called a **cylinder**. For example, the outermost track on the top side of a disk is called track 0, side 0, while the outermost track on the bottom side is called track 0, side 1. The combination of these two tracks is called cylinder 0.

The **disk controller** controls the read/write heads of a disk drive. Rather than reading and writing a single byte of data each time, the controller works with sectors and clusters. A **sector** is a 512 byte segment of data. Each sector is a wedge-shaped portion, resembling a piece of pie, that cuts across all tracks on one side. Because of the large number of sectors on a hard disk, the read/write heads access data in sector blocks called **clusters**. On a hard disk drive, a cluster may contain four to eight sectors. On a floppy diskette drive, one cluster is equal to one sector. A cluster is the smallest unit that the read/write heads retrieve or write to a disk.

Some of the more common disk specifications and capacities appear in Table 4.1. In the table, the abbreviation DS/DD is used for Double-Sided/ Double-Density and DS/HD is used for Double-Sided/High-Density. The primary difference between these two types of diskettes is the number of available sectors per track. DS/HD diskettes have more sectors per track, and therefore store more data than DS/DD diskettes. Although you must have a high-density disk drive in your computer to use DS/HD diskettes, DS/DD diskettes work in either double- or high-density disk drives. You can use the following formula to calculate the total number of bytes on a hard disk or floppy diskette:

Capacity = Tracks × Sides × Sectors per Track × 512 Bytes per Sector

Table 4.1	Disk	Tracks	Sectors Per Track	Bytes
Disk Statistics				
	5.25" DS/DD	40 (2 sides)	9	368,640 (360 KB)
	5.25" DS/HD	80 (2 sides)	15	1,228,800 (1.2 MB)
	3.5" DS/DD	80 (2 sides)	9	737,280 (720 KB)
	✴ 3.5" DS/HD	80 (2 sides)	18	1,474,560 – (1.44 MB)
	Hard Disks (one example)	682 (16 sides) *(8 disks)*	38	212,303,872 (212 MB)

Disks stacked on top of each other

DOUBLING A DISK'S CAPACITY

DOS 6 introduces a new program called DoubleSpace that compresses your program and data files to increase the available capacity on hard disks and floppy diskettes. On average, the DoubleSpace program results in 50 to 100 percent more free space being created on the target disk. To load

DoubleSpace and compress your disk drives, type DBLSPACE and press
(Enter) at the system prompt.

After the opening screen appears, you choose the Express Setup option to
compress the files on drive C: or the Custom Setup option to compress a
different disk drive. If you choose the Custom Setup option, you have the
option of compressing an existing drive or creating a newly compressed
drive. Compressing an existing drive may take upwards of an hour to
complete. Once you have compressed a drive, you use the DBLSPACE
command to retrieve information on the actual compression ratio and
estimated free disk space (Figure 4.1).

Figure 4.1

A DoubleSpace
information screen.

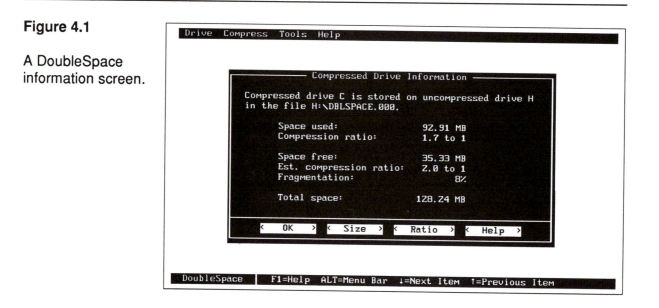

In this guide, we do not load the DoubleSpace program to compress a
drive because it significantly changes the computer's configuration. If your
computer has a compressed drive already, you can use the DBLSPACE
command to display compression statistics and defragment the drive. For
more information on using DoubleSpace, you should refer to the "Freeing
Disk Space" section in your MS-DOS 6 User's Guide.

(*Note*: At the time of this writing, Microsoft had lost a court battle to
include the DoubleSpace compression technology in DOS 6. Therefore, a
new release called DOS 6.21 is now being shipped without DoubleSpace.)

PREVENTIVE MAINTENANCE

Preventive maintenance involves planning and implementing procedures to prolong the operating life of your computer, ensure the stability of a disk, and safeguard important data. Before introducing the disk management commands, this section reviews some general practices for preventive maintenance.

PROTECTING YOUR COMPUTER

There are several precautions you can take to avoid mishaps and possible system failures. First, ensure that your computer is in a safe and secure location, away from major traffic areas in your home, school, or office. Bumping the computer while it is accessing the hard disk may damage the read/write heads, and sometimes the surface of the disk. Secondly, avoid placing the computer in areas with high concentrations of dust or smoke. Because the read/write heads of a floppy diskette drive rest on the surface of the diskette, dust or smoke particles on the surface can severely damage the heads.

Most importantly, protect your investment in a computer system with a power bar. One of the most devastating environmental hazards for a computer is dirty power, or the power fluctuations that occur in common wall sockets. *Do not connect the components of your computer directly to a wall socket.* Also, ensure that the power bar has surge suppression, and, preferably, a spike inhibitor. Lastly, do not mistake a $9.95 outlet bar for a proper power bar.

DEFRAGMENTING A DISK (DEFRAG)

As you store data on a new disk, DOS places the files in one contiguous block. If you subsequently delete one of these files, a gap appears on the disk. The next time you save a file, DOS fills the gap with as much of the new file as possible and then moves the remainder of the file to the end of the block. This file is now fragmented because its clusters are located in different areas on the disk.

File fragmentation is common on hard disks and causes the read/write heads to work much harder to retrieve and save files. Rather than moving to a single location to access a file, the read/write heads must travel to several places on the disk. As a result, a fragmented hard disk is slower to access and has a greater likelihood of disk failure.

To protect against fragmentation, DOS 6 provides a **disk optimizing** program called the Defragmenter. This program combines the individual clusters of a single file into one contiguous block and moves the unused space to the end of the data area, allowing new files to be appended to the end of the disk. By **defragmenting** the hard disk, you minimize the movement of the read/write heads and speed the transfer of data from the disk to RAM and the CPU.

The syntax for running the Microsoft Defragmenter is:

DEFRAG [*drive:*] [/F or /U] [/B] [/V]

where the switches do the following:

/F	Fully optimizes the disk; combines a file's individual clusters and moves the unused space to the end of the data area
/U	Unfragments files by combining their individual clusters, but does not move the unused space to the end of the data area
/B	Restarts the computer once it has finished defragmenting the specified disk
/V	Verifies that the fragmented file read into memory is correctly defragmented and written to the disk

Perform the following steps.

1. Ensure that the C:\> system prompt is displayed.

2. To fully optimize the Advantage Diskette:
    TYPE: defrag a: /f
    PRESS: [Enter]
    The following screen (Figure 4.2) appears briefly while the files on the diskette are reorganized.

Figure 4.2

Running the DOS 6 Defragmenter.

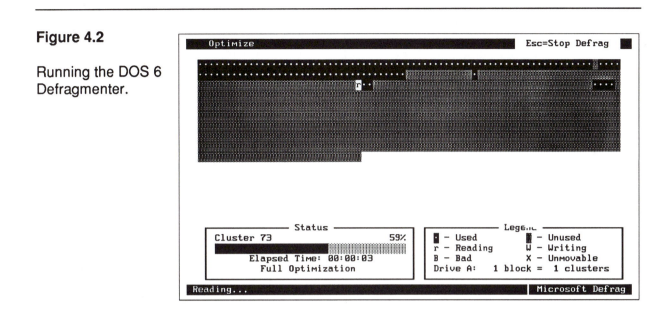

USING THE COMMAND LINE

This section introduces several disk management commands that you use to prepare new disks, duplicate disks, and protect against disk or system failures.

PREPARING A NEW DISK (FORMAT)

The FORMAT command prepares a new hard disk or floppy diskette for storing data by performing two functions: **physical formatting** and **logical formatting**. Physical formatting divides the disk into tracks, cylinders, and sectors, and gives each sector a unique address, similar to a post office box. Logical formatting organizes the disk into three primary areas: the **File Allocation Table (FAT)**, the root directory, and the data area. The

FAT contains the master index listing for all the program and data files on the disk. It is so important that DOS maintains two copies of the FAT. You cannot list the FAT using the DIR command or view the FAT using the TYPE command. It is a hidden system area, appearing on every disk, that enables DOS to store, locate, and retrieve files.

When you format a floppy diskette using the FORMAT command, DOS automatically performs a physical and logical format. For hard disks, however, the FORMAT command only performs a logical format. You use the DOS FDISK command to perform a physical format, sometimes called a low-level format, of a hard disk. As it is an advanced DOS command, FDISK is not covered in this guide.

The FORMAT command is often classified as a destructive command. In older versions of DOS, the FORMAT command erased the original information on the disk by overwriting the FAT, root directory, and data area. However, DOS 6 provides a safer formatting routine. In its default mode, the new FORMAT command only overwrites the FAT and the root directory—not the data area. This procedure is similar to erasing the table of contents and index of a book but leaving the pages intact. Although you cannot see the data after you format a disk, you can recover the files using DOS's UNFORMAT command.

The FORMAT command also checks the disk for **bad sectors**, except in the case of the Quick Format mode. A bad sector is an area of a disk that cannot reliably store information due to flaws in the magnetic coating. Hard disks almost always have some bad sectors; this should not be cause for alarm. Floppy diskettes, on the other hand, should be thrown away or returned to the manufacturer when bad sectors appear.

There are three formatting modes available for the FORMAT command:

1. *Safe Format mode (default mode)*
   The Safe Format mode erases the FAT and root directory of a previously formatted disk, and then checks the disk for bad sectors. You cannot use the Safe Format mode to format a new disk or to change a disk's capacity.

2. *Quick Format mode*
   The Quick Format mode is the fastest method for formatting a disk. Except for the bad sector check, the Quick Format mode performs the same steps as the Safe Format mode. You cannot use the Quick Format mode unless the disk has been previously formatted.

3. *Unconditional Format mode*
   The Unconditional Format mode is similar to the older versions of the FORMAT command. In this mode, the FAT, root directory, and data area are rebuilt. DOS uses the Unconditional Format mode to prepare a new disk or to change a disk's capacity.

You select the desired formatting mode using switches that accompany the FORMAT command. The syntax for the FORMAT command is as follows:

FORMAT *drive:* [/Q] [/U] [/F:*size*] [/S] [/V:*label*]

where the switches do the following:

/Q	Formats a disk using the Quick Format mode
/U	Formats a disk using the Unconditional Format mode
/F:*size*	Formats a diskette to a specific capacity, such as 360, 720, 1.2, 1.44, or 2.88 (for example, /F:720 or /F:1.44)
/S	Makes a DOS system diskette (a bootable diskette)
/V:*label*	Labels the formatted disk (for example, /V:DATA94)

Some examples of the FORMAT command appear below. ***Do not attempt these commands on your computer.***

a. To format a new diskette in drive A:, you would enter the following:
   TYPE: `format a:`
   PRESS: [Enter]
   (*Note*: Although the Safe Format mode is the default, new disks are automatically formatted using the Unconditional Format mode.)

b. To reformat a diskette in drive A: that contains existing information:
   TYPE: `format a: /q`
   PRESS: [Enter]
   The /Q switch employs the Quick Format mode, as shown in Figure 4.3.

Figure 4.3

Results of the
FORMAT command
with the /Q switch.

```
C:\>format a: /q
Insert new diskette for drive A:
and press ENTER when ready...

Checking existing disk format.
Saving UNFORMAT information.
QuickFormatting 1.44M
Format complete.

Volume label (11 characters, ENTER for none)?

    1,457,664 bytes total disk space
    1,457,664 bytes available on disk

         512 bytes in each allocation unit.
       2,847 allocation units available on disk.

Volume Serial Number is 3E59-1EE3

QuickFormat another (Y/N)?n


C:\>
```

c. To reformat a high-density 3.5" diskette to a double-density capacity:
    TYPE: format a: /f:720
    PRESS: [Enter]
    Although it is not a common practice, you may need to format a high-density diskette for use on a computer that only has a double-density diskette drive. (*Note*: When you change the capacity of a disk using the FORMAT command, DOS automatically uses the Unconditional Format mode.)

Quick Reference   Command: FORMAT (external)
FORMAT   Syntax: format [*drive:*] [/q] [/u] [/f:*size*] [/s] [/v:*label*]
Command   Purpose: Prepares or initializes a disk for storage

UNFORMATTING A DISK (UNFORMAT)

If you accidentally format a disk, you may be able to recover the data using the UNFORMAT command. Unfortunately, the UNFORMAT command does not work in every situation. For example, you cannot successfully unformat a disk in the following circumstances:

1. You formatted the disk using an earlier version of DOS.

2. You formatted the disk using the /U switch (Unconditional Format).

3. You formatted the disk to a new capacity using the /F:*size* switch.

To ensure that you can restore an accidentally formatted disk, you should always use the Safe Format mode or the Quick Format mode. The syntax for the UNFORMAT command is as follows:

UNFORMAT *drive:* [/L] [/TEST]

where the switches do the following:

/L	Lists all files and directories found on the formatted disk
/TEST	Displays information without actually unformatting the disk

Some examples of the UNFORMAT command appear below. ***Do not attempt these commands on your computer.***

a. To test the possibility of successfully unformatting a diskette in drive A:, you would do the following:
    TYPE: `unformat a: /test`
    PRESS: Enter
    Figure 4.4 shows an example of using the /TEST switch.

Figure 4.4

Using the
UNFORMAT
command to
restore files on
drive A:.

```
C:\>unformat a: /test

Insert disk to rebuild in drive A:
and press ENTER when ready.


  CAUTION !!
This attempts to recover all the files lost after a
format, assuming you've not been using the MIRROR command.
This method cannot guarantee complete recovery of your files.

The search-phase is safe: nothing is altered on the disk.
You will be prompted again before changes are written to the disk.

Using drive A:

Are you sure you want to do this?
If so, press Y; anything else cancels.
? N
```

b. To unformat a diskette in drive A:, listing all files and subdirectories:
    TYPE: unformat a: /l
    PRESS: [Enter]

....
Quick Reference   Command: UNFORMAT (external)
UNFORMAT   Syntax: unformat *drive:* [/l] [/test]
Command   Purpose: Restores an accidentally formatted disk
....

NAMING A DISK (VOL AND LABEL)

Using the LABEL command, you can attach an internal name (called a
volume label) to a disk that identifies its contents, as you would apply an
external label to a diskette. The LABEL command is also used to modify
and delete a volume label. To display the volume label and serial number
for a hard disk or floppy diskette, you use the VOL command.

The syntax for the VOL and LABEL commands follow:

VOL [*drive:*]

LABEL [*drive:*][*name*]

To practice naming a disk, perform the following steps.

1. Ensure that the Advantage Diskette is placed into drive A: and that the C:\> system prompt is displayed.

2. Move to drive A:.

3. To display the current volume label for the Advantage Diskette:
   TYPE: `vol`
   PRESS: `Enter`

4. To create a new volume label:
   TYPE: `label`
   PRESS: `Enter`

5. A label can contain up to 11 characters and can include spaces. To enter a new label name:
   TYPE: `work disk`
   PRESS: `Enter`

6. To display the volume label:
   TYPE: `vol`
   PRESS: `Enter`

7. To create another new volume label:
   TYPE: `label advantage`
   PRESS: `Enter`

8. TYPE: `dir /w`
   PRESS: `Enter`
   The volume label appears in the first line of a directory listing.

9. Clear the screen.

Quick Reference *VOL Command*	Command:	VOL (external)
	Syntax:	vol [*drive:*]
	Purpose:	Displays a drive's volume label and serial number

Quick Reference *LABEL Command*	Command:	LABEL (external)
	Syntax:	label [*drive:*][*name*]
	Purpose:	Creates, changes, and deletes a drive's volume label

CHECKING THE RELIABILITY OF A DISK (CHKDSK AND SCANDISK)

DOS 6 provides two programs called CHKDSK and ScanDisk for analyzing and repairing problems that occur with your disk's filing system. (*Note*: ScanDisk was introduced for the first time in DOS 6.2. Therefore, users with DOS 6.0 will not have this command.) The CHKDSK command, a carryover from previous DOS versions, reports and fixes common disk storage problems. For more in-depth disk analysis, you use the new ScanDisk program to check for logical and physical disk errors on regular and compressed drives. Frequent computer users should use CHKDSK or ScanDisk weekly to ensure the stability of their disks.

Some of the more common problems fixed by these programs are **lost clusters** and **cross-linked clusters**. A cluster is lost when it is marked in use by the FAT but is not part of a complete file. Lost clusters are usually the result of a power fluctuation in the middle of disk activity: before DOS can finish writing the entries in the FAT, it is interrupted by the power fluctuation and leaves one or more clusters behind. A cross-linked cluster is a segment of data that the FAT shows as belonging to more than one file. These problems are also caused by power fluctuations, so if the problems persist, ensure that you have a smooth electrical current from your wall socket. See the Preventive Maintenance section, Protecting Your Computer, earlier in this session.

The syntax for the CHKDSK command is as follows:

CHKDSK [*drive:*] [/F] [/V]

where the switches do the following:

/F   Fixes the errors found by the CHKDSK command; without
                this switch, CHKDSK only reports the errors it finds
/V   Provides a complete file listing as it checks the disk
                (the *V* stands for verbose; a listing of every file name)

The syntax for the ScanDisk program is as follows:

SCANDISK [*drive: or* /ALL]

Although there are multiple switches that you can use with the SCANDISK
command, it's easier to make selections from the prompts that appear once
the program loads. To begin checking all the drives on your computer, you
simply enter SCANDISK /ALL and then press (Enter).

To check the Advantage Diskette for errors, perform the following steps.

1. Ensure that the A:\> system prompt is displayed.

2. To run the CHKDSK program:
    TYPE: chkdsk
    PRESS: (Enter)

    After the CHKDSK command completes its analysis, a disk summary
    appears showing the total capacity, available capacity, number of
    directories, and number of user files on the disk. The last two lines in
    the summary show total conventional RAM and how much of it is
    available for programs.

    Your screen should now appear similar to Figure 4.5. (*Note*: Since the
    default drive is A:, you execute CHKDSK by simply typing the
    command and pressing (Enter). To check a disk other than the default
    or current disk drive, ensure that you include the drive letter in the
    command.)

Figure 4.5

Executing the
CHKDSK
program.

```
A:\>chkdsk

Volume ADVANTAGE    created 03-21-1994 11:48p
Volume Serial Number is 1049-1ADD

      730,112 bytes total disk space
        7,168 bytes in 7 directories
      115,712 bytes in 31 user files
      607,232 bytes available on disk

        1,024 bytes in each allocation unit
          713 total allocation units on disk
          593 available allocation units on disk

      655,360 total bytes memory
      582,816 bytes free

Instead of using CHKDSK, try using SCANDISK.  SCANDISK can reliably detect
and fix a much wider range of disk problems.  For more information,
type HELP SCANDISK from the command prompt.


A:\>
```

3. If CHKDSK reports errors, you execute the CHKDSK command again
    with the /F switch to correct those errors. For practice, run CHKDSK
    with the /F and /V switches:
    TYPE: chkdsk /f /v
    PRESS: [Enter]
    (*Note*: If you are using DOS 6.2, you must confirm the operation by
    typing y and pressing [Enter].)

4. If you are using DOS 6.2, you can also run the ScanDisk program:
    TYPE: scandisk
    PRESS: [Enter]
    Once the initial tests are completed, you are presented with the
    following screen in Figure 4.6.

Figure 4.6

Executing the
ScanDisk
program.

```
Microsoft ScanDisk

 ┌─────────────────────────────────────────────────────┐
 │ ScanDisk has finished testing the file structure of drive A. │
 │                                                       │
 │ If you want, ScanDisk can also perform a surface scan on this │
 │ drive. During a surface scan, ScanDisk checks the physical │
 │ surface of the disk and identifies any areas that may be │
 │ failing. In most cases, ScanDisk can recover the data from │
 │ such areas.                                           │
 │                                                       │
 │ A surface scan on drive A will take about 5 minutes. You can │
 │ stop the scan at any time by choosing Exit.           │
 │                                                       │
 │ Do you want to perform a surface scan now?            │
 │                                                       │
 │            ◄  Yes  ►    ‹  No  ›                       │
 └─────────────────────────────────────────────────────┘
```

5. To perform a physical surface scan of the diskette:
   CHOOSE: Yes command button
   This test may take several minutes, depending on the speed of your computer.

6. Assuming that there are no errors, exit the ScanDisk program when it has completed the surface scan:
   CHOOSE: Exit command button

Quick Reference | Command: | CHKDSK (external)
CHKDSK | Syntax: | chkdsk [*drive:*] [/f] [/v]
Command | Purpose: | Checks and verifies the readability of a disk

Quick Reference | Command: | SCANDISK (external)
SCANDISK | Syntax: | scandisk [*drive:* or /all]
Command | Purpose: | Analyzes and corrects problems with disks

Copying an Entire Diskette (DISKCOPY)

The DISKCOPY command duplicates an entire diskette. In contrast to the COPY command, DISKCOPY removes all the information on the target or destination drive to make the duplicate. In other words, DISKCOPY does not append files to the end of the destination diskette; it makes an exact copy of the original or source diskette. Therefore, the diskettes must be the same size and type to successfully produce a copy.

The syntax for the DISKCOPY command follows:

DISKCOPY *source destination* [/V]

The /V switch verifies the completeness and accuracy of the copied files, but requires more time to complete the duplication.

If you only have one diskette drive in your computer, the source and destination are the same drive letter and you must swap the original and target diskettes in and out of the drive to perform the copy. After entering the command (for example, `diskcopy a: a:`), you are prompted by DOS to place the original diskette in the drive. The information is read from the disk and stored in RAM. Then DOS asks you to swap the original diskette with the target diskette. The information is then written onto the new or target diskette.

DOS 6.2 greatly speeds the diskcopying process by enabling single-pass copying of high-density diskettes. In other words, you need to swap diskettes in and out of the drive only once to copy a high-density diskette.

Quick Reference	Command:	DISKCOPY (external)
DISKCOPY	Syntax:	diskcopy *source destination* [/v]
Command	Purpose:	Duplicates an entire diskette

Backing Up and Restoring Your Data Files (MSBACKUP)

Although the commands introduced in this session help prevent system failures, the most important safeguard to have is a backup of your data. Many computer users will attest that it is not a question of if your hard disk will fail, but when will it fail. In determining how often you need to perform a backup, you must decide how much work you are prepared to lose. If you back up your hard disk every four weeks, you must be prepared to lose one month's work. Having learned through experience, many computer users back up their hard disks on a daily basis.

DOS 6 introduces a new graphical backup and restore program called Microsoft Backup, which is available for both the MS-DOS and Windows environments. Using Microsoft Backup, you can copy files from your hard disk to floppy diskettes, restore files onto your hard disk after a system crash, and verify the accuracy of backed up information. Figure 4.7 shows the main program options: Backup, Restore, and Compare.

Figure 4.7

The Microsoft
Backup program.

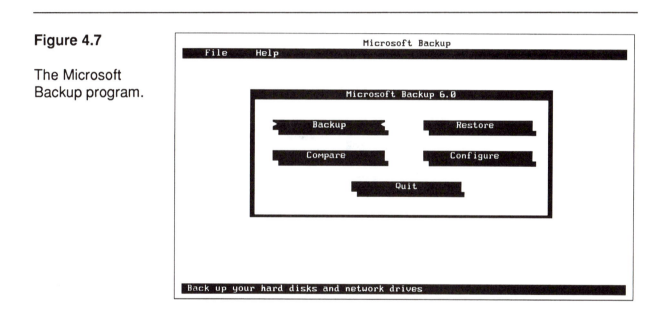

The syntax for loading the Microsoft Backup program is:

MSBACKUP [*setup file*]

where the setup file is an optional configuration file containing parameters for backing up your computer system. If you do not specify a settings file, MSBACKUP uses a default file called DEFAULT.SET.

Some examples of the MSBACKUP command appear below. *Do not attempt these commands on your computer.*

a. To load the Microsoft Backup program::
    TYPE: msbackup
    PRESS: (Enter)

b. To start a backup, do the following:
    CHOOSE: Backup command button
    The Backup screen appears as shown in Figure 4.8.

Figure 4.8

The Backup option in Microsoft Backup.

```
                          Microsoft Backup
     File     Help

                              Backup
     Setup File:
       DEFAULT.SET  (No Description)              start backup

                                                    Cancel
       Backup From        Backup To:
     ▶ [-C-]              MS-DOS Drive and Path
       [-H-]                                       Options...
                          [C:\DOS················]


       Select Files...    0 files selected for backup
                          0 K free space needed on MS-DOS drive

     Backup Type:
       Full

     Load a different setup file
```

c. CHOOSE: Select Files command button
    SELECT: *desired drives or files to back up*

d. CHOOSE: Backup To command button
    SELECT: *desired destination*

e. CHOOSE: Backup Type command button
SELECT: Full, Incremental, or Differential

There are three types of backups that you can perform:

Full Backup	Backs up selected files on the hard disk and flips each file's archive attribute to indicate that it has been backed up.
Incremental Backup	Backs up selected files on the hard disk that have been created or modified since the last full or incremental backup. An incremental backup flips the archive attribute for each file to indicate that it has been backed up.
Differential Backup	Backs up selected files on the hard disk that have been created or modified since the last full backup. A differential backup does not change a file's archive attribute.

You may decide, for example, to perform a full backup every Friday afternoon and a less time-consuming differential backup at the end of each business day. With these two backups, you will start every day with a full copy of your hard disk's files.

f. CHOOSE: Start Backup command button

Similarly to the process for backing up your data files, you use the MSBACKUP command to restore files to a hard disk that has been accidentally formatted, damaged by a power surge, or attacked by a computer virus. For more information on the MSBACKUP command, refer to "Managing Your System" in the MS-DOS 6 User's Guide.

Quick Reference
MSBACKUP
Command

Command:	MSBACKUP (external)
Syntax:	msbackup [*setup file*]
Purpose:	Backs up and restores your hard disk files

USING THE DOS SHELL

This section introduces the disk management commands that are available from the DOS Shell. In the Program List area, the Disk Utilities group contains program items for the DISKCOPY, FORMAT, and UNDELETE commands. To access the Disk Utilities group, highlight the item in the Program List area and press (Enter). Using a mouse, double-click on the Disk Utilities item. Figure 4.9 shows the program items that are available in the Disk Utilities group. The Backup and Restore items refer to the BACKUP and RESTORE commands that were available with earlier versions of DOS. To back up or restore files, use the MSBACKUP program discussed in the previous section.

Figure 4.9

The Disk Utilities program group.

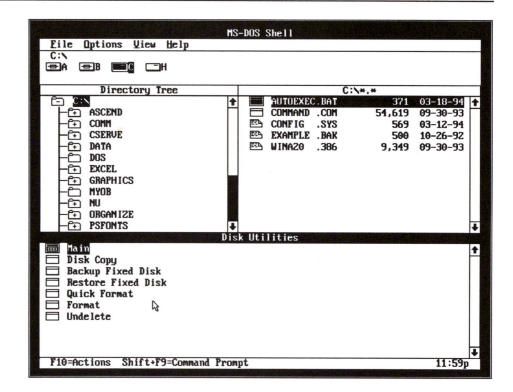

COPYING AN ENTIRE DISKETTE

To duplicate a diskette using the DOS Shell, choose Disk Copy from the Disk Utilities group. When prompted by the dialog box (Figure 4.10), you enter the source and destination parameters for the command. Although default parameters appear in the text box, you can type new parameters to replace the defaults. To proceed with the duplication, press (Enter) or click on OK. To abort the process, press (Esc) or click on the Cancel button. For further information on copying an entire disk, refer to the DISKCOPY command discussed earlier in this session.

Figure 4.10

The Disk Copy dialog box.

```
┌────────────────────────────────────────────────────────────────────┐
│                            MS-DOS Shell                              │
│   File  Options  View  Help                                          │
│   C:\                                                                │
│   ▭A    ▭B    ▬C    ▭H                                               │
│ ┌────────────────────┬─────────────────────────────────┬──────────┐ │
│ │                     │            Disk Copy            │03-18-94 ↑│ │
│ │ ┌─ C:\              │                                 │09-30-93  │ │
│ │ ├┤ A   Enter the source and destination drives.      │03-12-94  │ │
│ │ ├┤ C                                                  │10-26-92  │ │
│ │ ├┤ C                                                  │09-30-93  │ │
│ │ ├┤ D   Parameters . . .     a: b:                     │          │ │
│ │ ├┤ D                                                  │          │ │
│ │ ├┤ E      ( OK )      ( Cancel )      ( Help )         │          │ │
│ │ ├┤ G                                                  │          │ │
│ │ ├┤ MYOB                                               │          │ │
│ │ ├┤ NU                              ⬓                   │          │ │
│ │ ├┤ ORGANIZE                                           │          │ │
│ │ ├┤ PSFONTS              ↓         Disk Utilities      │          ↓│ │
│ ├─────────────────────────────────────────────────────────────────┤ │
│ │ ▤ Main                                                          ↑│ │
│ │ ▤ Disk Copy                                                      │ │
│ │ ▤ Backup Fixed Disk                                              │ │
│ │ ▤ Restore Fixed Disk                                             │ │
│ │ ▤ Quick Format                                                   │ │
│ │ ▤ Format                                                         │ │
│ │ ▤ Undelete                                                       │ │
│ │                                                                 ↓│ │
│ ├─────────────────────────────────────────────────────────────────┤ │
│   F10=Actions   Shift+F9=Command Prompt                      11:59p │
└────────────────────────────────────────────────────────────────────┘
```

Perform the following steps on your computer.

1. Ensure that the Advantage Diskette is placed into drive A: and that the A:\> system prompt is displayed.

2. Load the DOS Shell and change the view to Program/File Lists.

3. To display the program items for disk management:
   SELECT: Disk Utilities in the Program List area

4. To display the dialog box for the Disk Copy program item:
   SELECT: Disk Copy
   Your screen should now appear similar to Figure 4.10.

5. To return to the Disk Utilities group:
   PRESS: (Esc) or CLICK: Cancel

Quick Reference   1. Select the Disk Utilities group in the Program List area.
Copying an Entire   2. Select the Disk Copy program item.
Diskette   3. PRESS: Enter to proceed or CLICK: OK

FORMATTING A DISK

The Disk Utilities group provides two options for formatting a diskette. The Quick Format item formats a diskette using the Quick Format mode, while the Format item uses the default or Safe Format mode. When you select either item, a dialog box appears for you to enter or confirm the default parameters. To proceed, press Enter or click on OK. To abort the process, press Esc or click on the Cancel button. For more information on the available formatting modes, refer to the FORMAT command discussed earlier in this session.

Perform the following steps.

1. To display the dialog box for Quick Format:
   SELECT: Quick Format

2. To return to the Disk Utilities group:
   PRESS: Esc or CLICK: Cancel

3. Exit the DOS Shell.

Quick Reference   1. Select the Disk Utilities group in the Program List area.
Formatting a Disk   2. Select the Format or Quick Format program item.
                       3. PRESS: Enter to proceed or CLICK: OK

SUMMARY

This session introduced you to the DOS disk management commands. You learned the importance of preventive maintenance for avoiding mishaps and prolonging the life of your computer system and hard disk. The principles of disk storage were also discussed in this session, including the preparation of a new disk with physical and logical formatting. To safeguard your data files, you learned how to back up the hard disk.

The last few sections explored the disk management commands available from the DOS Shell. In the Program List area, the Disk Utilities group contains program items for duplicating and formatting a disk. Many of the commands and procedures appearing in this session are provided in the Command Summary (Table 4.2).

	Command	*Description*
Table 4.2		
	DBLSPACE	Increases the capacity of a disk through compression
Command Summary	DEFRAG	Optimizes a disk by defragmenting its files
	FORMAT	Prepares or initializes a disk
	UNFORMAT	Restores an accidentally formatted disk
	VOL	Displays a drive's volume label and serial number
	LABEL	Creates, changes, and deletes a drive's volume label
	CHKDSK	Checks and verifies the readability of a disk
	SCANDISK	Analyzes and corrects problems with disks
	DISKCOPY	Duplicates an entire diskette
	MSBACKUP	Backs up and restores your hard disk files
Disk Utilities Program Item	Disk Copy	Performs the DISKCOPY command
	Quick Format	Performs the FORMAT /Q command
	Format	Performs the FORMAT command

KEY TERMS

bad sector   An area of a disk that has flaws in its magnetic coating. Although bad sectors are commonly found on hard disks, a floppy diskette with bad sectors is unreliable and should not be used.

bit   A single digit of 1 or 0 in the binary number system, or machine language; a *byte* consists of 8 bits.

byte   The amount of space required to store a single character. A kilobyte is 1,024 bytes. A megabyte (MB) is approximately one million bytes, and a gigabyte (GB) is greater than one billion bytes.

clusters   A cluster consists of one or more sectors. Because there are too many sectors on a hard disk to manage efficiently, the disk controller groups sectors together to minimize the number of trips required by the read/write heads. On hard disks, there are typically four or eight sectors per cluster. On a floppy diskette, one cluster is equal to one sector.

cross-linked cluster   A cluster that is linked to two or more files, as recorded in the File Allocation Table (FAT). Cross-linked clusters are corrected using the CHKDSK /F command.

cylinder   The combination of two tracks that line up with each other on opposite sides of a disk. For example, cylinder 15 is the combination of track 15, side 0 and track 15, side 1.

defragmenting   The process of collecting, sorting, and rewriting files on a disk so that they appear in one contiguous block. Defragmenting a disk minimizes the movement required by the read/write heads.

disk controller   Hardware device that controls the read/write heads for the hard disk drive and the floppy diskette drives. The disk controller determines how many sectors are grouped together to form one cluster.

disk optimizing   See *defragmenting*.

File Allocation Table (FAT)   The master index of the disk. The FAT contains information on the location and relationships of each file on the disk. Because of its importance, there are two copies of the FAT.

file fragmentation   The situation where a single multiclustered file is stored in several different locations on a disk. File fragmentation slows a hard disk and requires the read/write heads to work harder, causing wear and tear on the components.

logical formatting   The formatting process that creates the File Allocation Table, root directory, and data area for a disk.

lost cluster   Cluster that is marked in use by the FAT, but does not belong to a complete file.

physical formatting   The formatting process that divides the disk into tracks, cylinders, and sectors, and gives each sector a unique address.

read/write head   Recording mechanism in magnetic storage devices, such as hard disks and floppy diskettes, that reads and writes the magnetic spots of data. Most disk drives have two read/write heads to access the top and bottom surfaces of a disk simultaneously.

sector   Wedge-shaped divisions on a disk; each sector stores 512 bytes of data. The intersection of a track and sector provides DOS with the location of data on a disk.

tracks   The concentric rings on the disk's surface where DOS stores data. The intersection of a track and sector provides DOS with the location of data on a disk.

EXERCISES

SHORT ANSWER

1. What is the capacity in megabytes of a hard disk with 613 tracks, 8 sides, and 17 sectors per track?
2. Why is a computer power bar necessary?
3. What is fragmentation? Is there a DOS command for optimizing a disk?
4. What are the three formatting modes?
5. How do you format a 5.25" double-density diskette in a 5.25" high-density disk drive?
6. What three circumstances prevent the UNFORMAT command from restoring an accidentally formatted disk?
7. What is the purpose of the DBLSPACE command?

8. Name the three main program options in Microsoft Backup.
9. Explain the three types of backups available in Microsoft Backup.
10. Where are the disk management commands located in the DOS Shell?

HANDS-ON

(*Note*: The commands introduced in this session can damage your computer if misused. Therefore, the hands-on exercises should be performed with a pen and paper, rather than on the computer. In the following exercises, you practice applying disk management commands in real-world situations.)

For the purpose of these exercises, imagine that your computer has one hard disk drive and two floppy diskette drives. Your hard disk's capacity is 80 MB, drive A: is a 5.25" high-density drive, and drive B: is a 3.5" high-density drive. Write down the correct form of each command, given that the C:\> system prompt is displayed on your computer.

1. The FORMAT command prepares new disks for storage or revitalizes existing disks. Write the commands that perform the following tasks:
   a. Format a new diskette in drive B:.
   b. Create a new DOS bootable diskette in drive A:. (*Hint*: Transfer the system files to the diskette using the FORMAT command.)
   c. Format an existing diskette in drive A: using the fastest mode.
   d. Format an existing diskette in drive B: and change the capacity from a high-density diskette to a double-density diskette.
   e. Format a new disk in drive B: and add a volume label called DATA.
   f. Format an existing diskette in drive A: using the fastest possible mode, and change the capacity from a high-density diskette to a double-density diskette.
   g. Format an existing diskette in drive A: using the Unconditional Format mode.

2. The UNFORMAT command restores a disk that has been accidentally formatted. Write the commands that perform the following tasks:
   a. List the files found on a recently formatted disk in drive A:.
   b. Unformat the diskette in drive A:.
   c. Test the possibility of unformatting a disk in drive B:.

3. The VOL and LABEL commands display and create a volume label for a disk. Write the commands that perform the following tasks:
   a. Display the volume label for drive A:.
   b. Display the volume label for drive B:.

   c. Create a volume label for drive A: called PROGRAMS.
   d. Create a volume label for drive B: called DATA.
   e. Erase the volume label for drive A:.
   f. Change the volume label for drive B: to WP6DATA.

4. The CHKDSK command reports and corrects disk and file errors. Write the commands that perform the following tasks:
   a. Check drive A: for disk errors.
   b. Assuming errors appeared on drive A:, correct the errors.
   c. Check drive B: for disk errors and provide a file listing.
   d. Assuming errors appeared on drive B:, correct the errors and provide a file listing.

5. The SCANDISK command analyzes and corrects logical and physical disk errors. Write the commands that perform the following tasks:
   a. Scan the disk in drive A: for errors.
   b. Scan all the disk drives in your computer.

6. The DISKCOPY command duplicates an entire diskette. Write the commands that perform the following tasks:
   a. Duplicate a 3.5" diskette.
   b. Duplicate a 5.25" diskette.

7. The DEFRAG command optimizes your hard disk by defragmenting files. Write the commands that perform the following tasks:
   a. Defragment your hard disk.
   b. Defragment a 3.5" diskette.

8. The DBLSPACE command compresses files to increase the capacity of your disk. Write the commands that perform the following tasks:
   a. Compress the files on your hard disk.
   b. Estimate the total storage capacity that will be available after running the DoubleSpace program.

DOS 6:
INCREASING YOUR PRODUCTIVITY

When first introduced, computers heralded the promise of greater efficiency and productivity for the common worker. However, more than one decade and 100 million personal computers later, most people have only begun to tap the processing potential of the personal computer. If you want to become a more productive computer user, you can use some of the advanced DOS tools introduced in this session.

PREVIEW

When you have completed this session, you will be able to:

Load the DOS Editor.

•

Create, modify, save, and print ASCII text files.

•

Create and execute a batch file program.

•

Record and execute command line macros.

•

Redirect the output of a command to another device.

•

Copy an entire directory structure.

•

Discuss memory management.

Why Is This Session Important?
Working with the DOS Text Editor (EDIT)
      The Guided Tour
      Moving Around a Text File
      Creating and Saving a File
      Opening an Existing File
      Printing a File
      Leaving the Editor
Using Batch Files
      Batch File Subcommands
      Creating and Using a Batch File
Using Macros (DOSKEY)
Customizing Your Computer
      The AUTOEXEC.BAT File
      The CONFIG.SYS File
Memory Management
      Types of Memory
      Memory Management Tools
      Displaying Memory Usage (MEM)
      Optimizing Memory (MEMMAKER)
      Displaying Technical Information (MSD)
Miscellaneous Commands
      Redirecting Input and Output
      Viewing the Contents of a File (MORE)
      Copying Files and Directories (XCOPY)
      Protecting Against Viruses (MSAV)
Summary
      Command Summary
Key Terms
Exercises
      Short Answer
      Hands-On

WHY IS THIS SESSION IMPORTANT?

This session introduces you to three main topics. First, you learn how to create and execute batch and system files using the DOS text editor. Second, the different types of memory and memory management programs are introduced. Lastly, you learn some miscellaneous commands that either enhance file and disk management operations or do not fit into one of the previous command categories discussed in this guide.

By the end of this session, you'll know how to use the following commands:

DOSKEY	MEMMAKER	MSD
EDIT	MORE	XCOPY
MEM	MSAV	

Before proceeding, make sure the following are true:

1. You have turned on your computer system and loaded DOS 6.
2. The C:\> system prompt is displayed on the screen.
3. Your Advantage Diskette is inserted into drive A:. You will work with files on the diskette that have been created for you. (*Note*: The Advantage Diskette can be duplicated by copying all of the files from your instructor's Master Advantage Diskette.)

WORKING WITH THE DOS TEXT EDITOR (EDIT)

The DOS Editor, first introduced in DOS 5.0, enables you to create, save, and print batch files (BAT), system files (SYS), and other ASCII text files. The Editor is not a full-featured word processing software program that you would use for writing reports or novels. You cannot format documents with fonts, headers and footers, or custom page layouts. Rather, the Editor is designed to create simple text files consisting of line item entries. When compared to the EDLIN line editor included with earlier versions of DOS, the full-screen Editor is much easier to use.

You start the Editor from the command line or the DOS Shell. From the DOS Shell, select the Editor item in the Program List area. From the command line, you enter the EDIT command using the following syntax:

EDIT [*file name*]

(*Note*: The DOS Editor requires two program files called EDIT.COM and QBASIC.EXE. If you have problems starting the Editor, verify that both of these files exist in the current directory or the DOS search path.)

When you use the EDIT command without a file name, the Editor is loaded into memory and presents an introductory message screen (Figure 5.1). To view further instructions on how to use the Editor, press the [Enter] key. To proceed to a blank document screen, press the [Esc] key. If you start the Editor by entering a file name after the EDIT command, the Editor is loaded into memory and immediately searches for the file. If the file is found, the Editor opens the file for editing. If the file is not found, the Editor creates a blank document and places the file name in the Title bar.

Figure 5.1

The DOS Editor
program screen.

```
 File  Edit  Search  Options                                   Help
                          Untitled

             ┌──────────────────────────────────────┐
             │        Welcome to the MS-DOS Editor        │
             │                                        │
             │  Copyright (C) Microsoft Corporation, 1987-1992.  │
             │          All rights reserved.          │
             │  ‹ Press Enter to see the Survival Guide ›  │
             ├──────────────────────────────────────┤
             │  ‹ Press ESC to clear this dialog box ›  │
             └──────────────────────────────────────┘



 F1=Help    Enter=Execute    Esc=Cancel    Tab=Next Field    Arrow=Next Item
```

Perform the following steps:

1. Ensure that the Advantage Diskette is placed into drive A: and that the A:\> system prompt is displayed.

2. To load the Editor:
    TYPE: edit
    PRESS: [Enter]

3. To proceed to the document screen:
   PRESS: Esc

Quick Reference   From the command line:
Loading the DOS   Command: EDIT (external)
Editor   Syntax: edit [*file name*]
                       Purpose: Loads the DOS Editor for creating and saving text files

                       From the DOS Shell:
                       a. Select the Program List area.
                       b. Select the Main Program group.
                       c. Select the Editor program item.

THE GUIDED TOUR

After loading the Editor and bypassing the Help information, a blank document appears with the word "Untitled" at the top of the screen. Until you save your work to the disk, this file remains untitled. Take a few minutes to familiarize yourself with the screen. The Editor groups commands together on the Menu bar, located at the top of the screen. You execute commands from the Editor Menu bar in the same way that you choose commands in the DOS Shell.

At the bottom and right-hand side of the screen, the Editor provides horizontal and vertical scroll bars. Using a mouse, you click the arrow appearing at the top or bottom of the vertical scroll bar to move one line up or down in the file. You click the arrow appearing at the left- or right-hand side of the horizontal scroll bar to move one column left or right. The current line and column number appear in the Status bar, in the bottom right-hand corner of the screen. In addition, the Status bar provides editing information, including available commands, helpful messages, and the current key lock status.

MOVING AROUND A TEXT FILE

There are better ways for moving around a file than pressing the ↑ and ↓ cursor-movement keys. Although these keystrokes work well when there are only a few lines on the screen, you cannot easily move through a 50-page programming source file with these keystrokes. Table 5.1 shows some of the cursor-movement and editing keys.

Table 5.1	*Keyboard*	*Description*
Cursor-Movement Keys	↑ and ↓	Moves the cursor up or down one line
	← and →	Moves the cursor to the previous or next character
	Ctrl + ←	Moves the cursor to the beginning of the previous word
	Ctrl + →	Moves the cursor to the beginning of the next word
	PgUp	Moves the cursor up one screen
	PgDn	Moves the cursor down one screen
	Home	Moves to the beginning of the current line
	End	Moves to the end of the current line
	Ctrl + Home	Moves to the beginning of the document or file
	Ctrl + End	Moves to the end of the document or file
Editing Keys	BackSpace	Deletes the character to the left of the cursor
	Delete	Deletes the character at the current cursor position
	Ctrl + t	Deletes the word at the cursor

CREATING AND SAVING A FILE

Creating a text file using the DOS Editor is easy. You type the information onto the screen and then save the document to the disk. Before entering text into the file, make sure that you have a blinking cursor in the upper left-hand corner of the screen. This marks the location where text is inserted.

To illustrate the fundamentals of inserting and deleting text, perform the following steps.

1. Make sure that you have loaded the Editor and that a cursor appears near the top left-hand corner of the screen.

2. TYPE: `list`
   The cursor appears one character to the right of the word *list*.

3. To move the cursor back to the beginning of the line:
   PRESS: [Home]
   The cursor appears under the letter *l* in *list*.

4. TYPE: `to do`
   PRESS: Space Bar
   As you type, the existing information is pushed to the right.

5. To move the cursor to the end of the line:
   PRESS: [End]

6. To add a couple of blank lines:
   PRESS: [Enter] twice

7. TYPE: `1. Pick up laundry`
   PRESS: [Enter]

8. TYPE: `2. Go shopping`
   PRESS: [Enter]

9. TYPE: `3. Book a squash court`
   PRESS: [Enter]

10. To move to the top of the file:
    PRESS: [Ctrl]+[Home]

11. To save the file to the Advantage Diskette:
    CHOOSE: File, Save As
    (*Note*: To save a file to the disk, you can choose the File, Save or File, Save As command from the Menu bar. These commands are identical if the document has never been saved before. Otherwise, you use the File, Save As command only when you want to change the name of a file or to save the file to a different location.)

12. TYPE: `a:todolist.txt`
    PRESS: [Enter]
    Notice that the title at the top of the screen now displays the file name.

1.   CHOOSE: <u>F</u>ile, <u>S</u>ave or <u>F</u>ile, Save <u>A</u>s from the Menu bar
2.   If the file has never been saved before, enter the file name.
                      3.   PRESS: (Enter) or CLICK: OK

OPENING AN EXISTING FILE

To modify or print an existing file, you must first retrieve the file from storage using the <u>F</u>ile, <u>O</u>pen command. Once the Open dialog box is displayed, type the full name of the file or enter the *.* wildcard file specification to list all the files. If you use the *.* file specification, the file list box displays all the files in the current directory. Highlight the desired file in the list box and then press (Enter).

Perform the following steps.

1.   To open an existing file:
     CHOOSE: <u>F</u>ile, <u>O</u>pen

2.   To move to the Files list box using the keyboard:
     PRESS: (Tab)

3.   To open the EXAMPLE.TXT file:
     SELECT: EXAMPLE.TXT file
     PRESS: (Enter)
     Select the file with the cursor-movement keys and press (Enter) or double-click on the file using the mouse. The file is selected when it appears highlighted.

4.   To open a different file:
     CHOOSE: <u>F</u>ile, <u>O</u>pen

5.   To list all the files in the current directory and not just the files with a TXT extension:
     TYPE: * . * in the File Name box
     PRESS: (Enter)
     All the files on the Advantage Diskette appear in the Files list box (Figure 5.2).

Figure 5.2

The Open dialog box with all files listed in the File list box.

```
■  File  Edit  Search  Options                                    Help
                              EXAMPLE.TXT
This │                           Open
for t │
text  │  File Name:  ■.■                                      ▮
creat │
Micro │  A:\
and d │                      Files                   Dirs/Drives
text  │
      │  BILLS.WK1    HARDWARE.ASC  SALES.MAR    123DATA      ↑
      │  BUDGET       HARDWARE.TXT  SALES.WK1    DB4DATA
      │  BUDGET.WK1   INCOME.WK1    SEMINAR.LET  PROGRAMS
      │  CASH.XLS     NAMES         SOFTWARE.1   WP6DATA
      │  EMPLOYEE.WK1 Q1.WK1        SOFTWARE.4   [-A-]
      │  EXAMPLE.TXT  Q2.WK1        STATS.XLS    [-B-]
      │  EXPENSES.DBF Q3.WK1        SUMMARY.WK1  [-C-]
      │  HARDWARE     Q4.WK1        TODOLIST.TXT [-H-]    ↓
      │
      │        < OK >            < Cancel >         < Help >

 ■
 F1=Help    Enter=Execute   Esc=Cancel   Tab=Next Field   Arrow=Next Item
```

6. SELECT: HARDWARE.ASC file
    PRESS: (Enter)

Quick Reference
Opening an
Existing File

1. CHOOSE: File, Open from the Menu bar
2. Type the file name to retrieve or select the file from the Files list box.
3. PRESS: (Enter) or CLICK: OK

PRINTING A FILE

To print the currently displayed text file, choose the File, Print command from the Menu bar. The Editor allows you to print a selected area of text in the file or the entire document. Using the keyboard, you select an area of text by holding down the (Shift) key and then pressing the cursor-movement keys. Using the mouse, you select a section of text by dragging the mouse pointer over the desired area.

Perform the following steps.

1. To print a section of text, first move the cursor to the top of the file:
   PRESS: [Ctrl]+[Home]

2. To select the first two paragraphs in the HARDWARE file:
   PRESS: [Shift] and hold it down
   PRESS: [↓] nine times
   Make sure that the first two paragraphs are highlighted before proceeding to the next step.

3. To print the selected area:
   CHOOSE: File, Print

4. SELECT: Selected Text Only
   PRESS: [Enter]
   The highlighted section of text is sent to the printer.

5. To print the entire file:
   CHOOSE: File, Print

6. SELECT: Complete Document
   PRESS: [Enter] or CLICK: OK

....

Quick Reference   1. CHOOSE: File, Print from the Menu bar
Printing a Text File   2. Select whether to print only a selected area of text or the entire
        document.
     3. PRESS: [Enter] or CLICK: OK

....

LEAVING THE EDITOR

When you are finished using the Editor, save your work and exit the program before turning off the computer. If you have made modifications to a file and have not yet saved the changes, the Editor will ask whether the file should be saved or abandoned before exiting the program (Figure 5.3).

Figure 5.3

Leaving the DOS
Editor program.

```
 ■  File  Edit  Search  Options                                    Help
                        ┌─── HARDWARE.ASC ───┐
Computer systems should be kept in an environment with a constant temperature.▐▌
Microcomputers tend to have the most system failures in colder climates, where
office temperatures are often controlled by automatic thermostats. These
thermostats stabilize warm temperatures during the day, but allow cool
temperatures at night.

The ideal temperature for microcomputers ranges from 60 to 90 degrees
Fahrenheit when ┌──────────────────────────────────────────┐grees when the
system is off.  │                                          │
               │   Loaded file is not saved. Save it now? │
But maintaining│                                          │re important
than the number│                                          │lly occur if a
microcomputer sy│  < Yes >   <  No  >   <Cancel>   < Help >│mperature in
short amounts of└──────────────────────────────────────────┘

The chips inside the system unit can work their way out their sockets in the
system boards. In addition the chip connectors can corrode more quickly so
that they become brittle and crack.

Hard disks suffer from dramatic changes in temperature, which can cause   ■
read/write problems. If a new hard disk drive has been shipped in a cold
─────────────────────────────────────────────────────────────────────────────
 ■
 F1=Help    Enter=Execute    Esc=Cancel    Tab=Next Field    Arrow=Next Item
```

Perform the following steps.

1. To exit the DOS Editor:
    CHOOSE: File, Exit

2. If you have made any modifications to the file, a dialog box appears. To
    abort the modifications and exit:
    SELECT: No

Quick Reference
*Exiting the DOS
Editor*

1. CHOOSE: File, Exit from the Menu bar
2. If necessary, respond to the prompts for saving or aborting the
    document text file, or choose to cancel the command altogether.

USING BATCH FILES

Most people perform repetitive activities with their computer. Whether
moving files from one location to another or loading an application
software program, you often enter several repetitive DOS commands.

Rather than performing the same commands each time, you can store the commands in a special program file called a **batch file**. To execute these commands, you type the file name of the batch file at the system prompt. DOS reads and executes each command line that is stored in the batch file, and then returns you to the system prompt. Batch files automate frequently performed tasks, making your computer easier to use for yourself and others.

A batch file is a text file containing a collection of DOS commands. You create, modify, and save batch files using the DOS Editor. Every batch file must have a BAT extension to inform DOS that it is a program file. You can avoid confusion by never naming a batch file after an existing DOS command. If program files have the same file name, DOS processes the files based on their extension: first COM files, then EXE files, and lastly, BAT files. For example, if DOS finds a FORMAT.COM file and a FORMAT.BAT file in the same directory, the FORMAT.COM file is executed when you type FORMAT at the system prompt. If necessary, you can override this pecking order of commands by typing the entire file name at the system prompt, such as FORMAT.BAT, before pressing (Enter).

BATCH FILE SUBCOMMANDS

A batch file can contain any of the DOS commands that you have learned in this guide. In addition to these regular DOS commands, there are several specially designed commands for batch files. The most popular batch file subcommands are ECHO and ECHO OFF, PAUSE, and REM. You should only use these commands in batch files—do not enter these commands at the system prompt. A description of each command appears in Table 5.2.

Table 5.2	*Command*	*Description*
Batch File Subcommands	ECHO OFF	During execution, ECHO OFF stops DOS from displaying each command listed in the batch file
	ECHO	After using ECHO OFF, you must use the ECHO command to display messages to the screen
	PAUSE	Temporarily stops the batch file until a key is pressed
	REM	Annotates your batch file with remarks that are not processed by DOS

Creating and Using a Batch File

In this section, you create a simple batch file using the DOS Editor. This batch file displays several directory listings using various forms of the DIR command. To create the batch file, perform the following steps.

1. Ensure that the A:\> system prompt is displayed.

2. To create a batch file called LISTING.BAT, you load the DOS Editor:
    TYPE: `edit listing.bat`
    PRESS: [Enter]

3. With the cursor positioned in the top left-hand corner of the Editor screen, you start typing in the commands that will appear in the batch file. To insert the first line in LISTING.BAT:
    TYPE: `echo off`
    PRESS: [Enter]
    You use ECHO OFF as the first line to turn off the screen display of subsequent commands in the batch file. The results of a command are displayed, but the command itself is not displayed. To turn off the display of the ECHO OFF command, you can precede it with the @ symbol (for example, @ECHO OFF).

4. To place a remark in the batch file for documentation, enter the REM command followed by a comment:
    TYPE: `rem This is a test batch file program`
    PRESS: [Enter]

5. In most batch files, you clear the screen before executing commands:
    TYPE: `cls`
    PRESS: [Enter]

6. To have the batch file perform a basic directory listing:
    TYPE: `dir`
    PRESS: [Enter]

7. Before clearing the screen again, you will pause the batch file so that the information stays on the screen until a key is pressed. Insert the PAUSE command:
    TYPE: `pause`
    PRESS: [Enter]

8. TYPE: `cls`
    PRESS: [Enter]

9. To send a message to the screen during the execution of this batch file:
   TYPE: echo Now another directory listing
   PRESS: (Enter)

10. Insert a command to pause the batch file again:
    TYPE: pause
    PRESS: (Enter)

11. To have the batch file list a directory across the width of the screen, insert the DIR command with the /W switch:
    TYPE: dir /w
    PRESS: (Enter)

12. TYPE: pause
    PRESS: (Enter)

13. Clear the screen for the last time:
    TYPE: cls
    PRESS: (Enter)
    Your Editor screen should now appear similar to Figure 5.4.

Figure 5.4

The LISTING batch file.

```
 File  Edit  Search  Options                                    Help
┌──────────────────────── LISTING.BAT ────────────────────────┐
│echo off                                                      │
│rem This is a test batch file program                         │
│cls                                                           │
│dir                                                           │
│pause                                                         │
│cls                                                           │
│echo Now another directory listing                            │
│pause                                                         │
│dir /w                                                        │
│pause .                                                       │
│cls                                                           │
│                                                              │
│                                                              │
│                                                              │
│                                                              │
│                                                              │
│                                                              │
│                                                              │
│                                                              │
│                                                              │
│                                                              │
MS-DOS Editor  <F1=Help> Press ALT to activate menus         00012:001
```

14. To save the LISTING.BAT batch file to the disk:
    CHOOSE: File, Save

15. To exit the DOS Editor:
    CHOOSE: File, Exit

16. To execute the batch file, you type its file name at the system prompt:
    TYPE: listing
    PRESS: (Enter)
    Notice that the batch file stops at each pause statement. Continue processing the batch file by pressing a key when prompted.

    CAUTION: If a batch file is not executing correctly, press (Ctrl)+c to stop the program. The message "Terminate batch job (Y/N)?" appears. To end the program, type y and then press (Enter). To continue the program, type n and then press (Enter).

USING MACROS (DOSKEY)

Whereas a batch file is a collection of DOS commands stored in a disk file, a **macro** is a collection of commands stored in RAM. Because a computer can access RAM much faster than a disk, macros execute faster than batch files. However, they are erased when the computer's power is turned off. You create a macro using the DOSKEY command. In addition to macros, DOSKEY enables you to store commands entered at the system prompt for later recall, editing, or execution. When the DOSKEY memory area becomes full, the first command stored is discarded to make room for the last command entered.

You install DOSKEY into memory as a TSR (terminate-stay-resident) program using the following syntax:

DOSKEY [/REINSTALL] [/MACROS] [/HISTORY]
        [MACRONAME=[*commands*]]

where the switches do the following:

/REINSTALL	Reinstalls a new copy of DOSKEY in memory
/MACROS	Displays macros stored in memory
/HISTORY	Displays commands stored in memory
MACRONAME	Creates a macro

The DOSKEY command is typically placed in the AUTOEXEC.BAT file. Once it is installed, you use the DOSKEY keystrokes listed in Table 5.3 to recall, search, and manipulate the commands stored in memory.

Table 5.3	*Keystroke*	*Description*
DOSKEY Keystrokes	⬆	Displays last command added to list
	⬇	Displays next command in list
	PgUp	Displays oldest command
	PgDn	Displays newest command
	Esc	Erases the displayed command
	F7	Lists all commands stored in memory
	Alt+F7	Erases the commands stored in memory
	F8	Searches for a command in the list
	F9	Specifies a command in the list
	Alt+F10	Erases the macros stored in memory

To practice using the DOSKEY command, perform the following steps from the A:\> system prompt.

1. To load the DOSKEY program into memory:
    TYPE: doskey
    PRESS: Enter

2. To illustrate how DOSKEY records commands, enter the following six commands:
   TYPE: dir /p
   PRESS: [Enter]
   TYPE: cls
   PRESS: [Enter]
   TYPE: dir *.* /oe /w
   PRESS: [Enter]
   TYPE: ver
   PRESS: [Enter]
   TYPE: attrib *.*
   PRESS: [Enter]
   TYPE: dir
   PRESS: [Enter]

3. To recall the VER command:
   PRESS: [↑] three times
   PRESS: [Enter]

4. To list all the commands stored in memory:
   PRESS: [F7]
   Your screen should appear similar, but not identical, to Figure 5.5.

Figure 5.5

Listing the commands stored in memory by DOSKEY.

```
Q3        WK1      2,259 08-08-91  12:00p
Q4        WK1      2,258 08-08-91  12:00p
SALES     WK1      2,655 08-08-91  12:00p
SUMMARY   WK1      2,826 08-08-91  12:00p
CASH      XLS      6,265 08-31-92  12:00p
STATS     XLS      2,246 08-31-92  12:00p
TODOLIST  TXT         77 03-22-94  12:13a
LISTING   BAT        136 03-22-94  12:20a
       37 file(s)     102,093 bytes
                      605,184 bytes free

A:\>ver

MS-DOS Version 6.20


A:\>
1: dir /p
2: cls
3: dir *.* /oe /w
4: ver
5: attrib *.*
6: dir
7: ver
A:\>
```

5. To execute the ATTRIB command again:
   PRESS: F9
   TYPE: *the line number with the ATTRIB command (in Figure 5.5, line 5 shows the ATTRIB command)*
   PRESS: Enter *twice*
   You should always press F7 to display the current line numbers before issuing the F9 command.

6. To search for a command:
   TYPE: dir
   PRESS: F8 *several times*
   Notice that the F8 key cycles through the commands that begin with the letters *dir*.

7. To remove the command appearing at the system prompt:
   PRESS: Esc

8. To create a DOSKEY macro, you enter the name of the macro followed by an equal sign, and then type the desired commands. Create a macro that displays a directory sorted by file name:
   TYPE: doskey byname=cls $t dir /on /p
   PRESS: Enter
   The "$t" separates the CLS command from the DIR command. Whenever you have more than one command in a macro, "$t" must separate each command. Each macro can store a maximum of 127 characters.

9. To list all the macros stored in memory:
   TYPE: doskey /macros
   PRESS: Enter

10. To execute the macro:
    TYPE: byname
    PRESS: Enter

Because macros are discarded when the computer's power is turned off, you should create a batch file that automatically loads all your macros. One method for creating a batch file is to redirect the output from the DOSKEY /MACROS command to a disk file. Using the DOS Editor, you modify the file by placing the DOSKEY command before each of the listed macros and then save the file. After that, whenever you want to load your macros, you simply execute the batch file.

Perform the following steps to create a batch file that loads macros.

1. To create the initial macro batch file:
   TYPE: doskey /macros > macros.bat
   PRESS: (Enter)
   The output redirection symbol (>) is explained later in this session.

2. To edit the batch file:
   TYPE: edit macros.bat
   PRESS: (Enter)

3. You must prefix the first line with the word DOSKEY, because the command to create a macro is DOSKEY *macroname=commands*:
   TYPE: doskey
   PRESS: Space Bar

4. To save the MACROS.BAT file and exit the DOS Editor:
   CHOOSE: File, Save
   CHOOSE: File, Exit

5. To load the macro contained in the macros file:
   TYPE: macros
   PRESS: (Enter)

6. Clear the screen.

....

Quick Reference	Command:	DOSKEY (external)
DOSKEY	Syntax:	doskey [/reinstall] [/macros] [/history]
Command		[*macroname=[commands]*]
	Purpose:	Recalls and edits DOS commands, and creates macros

....

CUSTOMIZING YOUR COMPUTER

After you boot the computer, DOS searches the root directory of the boot drive for the AUTOEXEC.BAT file and the CONFIG.SYS file—two files that you create and modify using the DOS Editor. The instructions contained in these files configure the computing environment and perform repetitive startup tasks.

THE AUTOEXEC.BAT FILE

The AUTOEXEC.BAT file is a batch file that automatically executes each time the computer is booted. As discussed in several sections of this guide, there are certain commands that should be executed each time you use the computer. Rather than entering these commands yourself, you place them in the AUTOEXEC.BAT file. The last instruction in this file typically calls a menu program, the DOS Shell, or Microsoft Windows.

Some of the more common DOS commands that appear in the AUTOEXEC.BAT file are summarized in Table 5.4.

Table 5.4	*Command*	*Description*
DOS Commands Typically Found in AUTOEXEC.BAT	PROMPT	Specifies the system prompt; for example, PROMPT PG
	PATH	Specifies the search path; for example, PATH C:\;C:\DOS
	DOSKEY	Loads the DOSKEY program
	DOSSHELL	Loads the DOS Shell (usually the last command in the file)

THE CONFIG.SYS FILE

The CONFIG.SYS file is a text file that contains special configuration commands. These commands often control hardware devices that are attached to your computer, such as a mouse or an atypical video display. Many application software programs specify certain command settings that must appear in the CONFIG.SYS file for the software to run properly. In some cases, the installation process for a software program automatically updates the CONFIG.SYS file with the necessary settings. Otherwise, you modify the CONFIG.SYS file using the DOS Editor.

If the changes that you make to the CONFIG.SYS and AUTOEXEC.BAT files cause your computer to behave erratically, you can bypass them at startup by pressing F5 when the "Starting MS-DOS..." message appears. If you want to skip only a few commands, you press F8 to tell DOS you want to confirm each command on a line-by-line basis. Once finished with the CONFIG.SYS file, DOS displays the message "Process AUTOEXEC.BAT [Y, N]?" and awaits your confirmation.

Another new feature in DOS 6 is the ability to create and select from multiple system configurations using a single CONFIG.SYS file. Since the commands for achieving this are more advanced than the topics covered in this guide, please refer to Configuring Your System in the MS-DOS 6 User's Guide for a detailed discussion.

MEMORY MANAGEMENT

This section explains the different types of memory and memory management techniques. You will also learn the DOS memory management tools that allow you to optimize your system's available memory.

TYPES OF MEMORY

There are two primary types of memory, ROM and RAM. **ROM** is read-only memory and contains the instructions for the basic input and output operations of the computer. These instructions are permanently encoded onto special chips. **RAM,** or random-access memory, is volatile memory and provides the interactive work area for your programs and data. RAM is divided into conventional, upper, extended, and expanded memory.

Conventional memory makes up the area from 0 KB to 640 KB in RAM. This memory area provides the workspace for the majority of your programs and data. The memory area between 640 KB and 1 MB is called the **upper memory** area or reserved memory. This area is reserved for managing various hardware devices, such as a graphics adapter.

Extended memory exists above the 1 MB address space. A memory manager, such as HIMEM.SYS, is required to access extended memory. The first 64 KB block of extended memory is called the **High Memory Area (HMA)**. DOS 6 takes advantage of computers with extended memory by loading some operating system instructions into the HMA. This frees up space in conventional memory for your programs and data.

Expanded memory usually refers to a memory board that you add to your computer. However, you can use extended memory to emulate expanded memory with the proper software. Although once popular, expanded memory is now used by relatively few programs.

MEMORY MANAGEMENT TOOLS

DOS provides two memory management programs, HIMEM.SYS and EMM386.EXE. These programs are loaded from the CONFIG.SYS file when you boot the computer. The HIMEM.SYS program enables programs to access extended memory. The EMM386.EXE program uses extended memory to emulate expanded memory on computers with an 80386 or higher processor. It also manages the upper memory area between 640 KB and 1 MB. To load these programs, you would place the following two lines into the CONFIG.SYS file:

```
DEVICE=HIMEM.SYS
DEVICE=EMM386.EXE
```

To free up conventional memory, you can load part of the DOS 6 operating system into extended memory and some device drivers into upper memory. To load DOS into high memory, you would place the following statement after the HIMEM.SYS and EMM386.EXE statements:

```
DOS=HIGH
```

These programs contain several options that are beyond the discussion in this guide. Refer to the MS-DOS 6 User's Guide if you need further information on customizing your computer.

DISPLAYING MEMORY USAGE (MEM)

Memory management refers to the way DOS allows applications to access the computer's memory. To see how memory is allocated in your computer you use the MEM command. MEM displays the amount of used and unused conventional, extended, and expanded memory.

The syntax for the MEM command follows:

MEM [/C] [/D] [/P]

where the switches do the following:

/C	Displays memory locations of programs that are loaded into memory (also /CLASSIFY)
/D	Displays memory information for programmers (/DEBUG)
/P	Displays one page of information at a time

Perform the following steps.

1. To view a basic memory report:
   TYPE: mem
   PRESS: [Enter]
   Your screen should appear similar, but not identical, to Figure 5.6.

Figure 5.6

The MEM command.

```
A:\>mem

Memory Type        Total   =    Used   +    Free
----------------   -------      -------     -------
Conventional        640K         75K        565K
Upper               155K         81K         74K
Reserved            384K        384K          0K
Extended (XMS)    2,917K      2,265K        652K
----------------   -------      -------     -------
Total memory      4,096K      2,805K      1,291K

Total under 1 MB    795K        156K        639K

Largest executable program size        565K  (578,496 bytes)
Largest free upper memory block         42K   (42,528 bytes)
MS-DOS is resident in the high memory area.

A:\>
```

2. To view a memory report using the /CLASSIFY switch:
   TYPE: mem /c /p
   PRESS: [Enter]
   PRESS: Space Bar to continue

3. To view a programmer's reference for memory:
   TYPE: mem /d /p
   PRESS: [Enter]
   PRESS: Space Bar repeatedly until the system prompt appears

---

Quick Reference
MEM Command

Command:	MEM (external)
Syntax:	mem [/c] [/d] [/p]
Purpose:	Displays memory information for your computer

OPTIMIZING MEMORY (MEMMAKER)

In earlier versions of DOS, you all but required a degree in computer programming to understand the means for optimizing memory. With the introduction of MemMaker in DOS 6, now even novice users can fine-tune their computer's memory usage. On 80386 and higher computers, MemMaker frees up conventional memory for your application software programs by moving device drivers and TSR programs into the upper memory area. The syntax for the MemMaker command is as follows:

MEMMAKER [/BATCH or /UNDO]

where the switches do the following:

/BATCH   Runs MemMaker without displaying any prompts
/UNDO   Removes   the   changes   last   made   to   your
                    CONFIG.SYS and AUTOEXEC.BAT files

An example of the MEMMAKER command appears below. ***Do not attempt these commands on your computer.***

a. To load the MemMaker program in interactive mode (as opposed to batch mode with the /BATCH switch):
    TYPE: `memmaker`
    PRESS: (Enter)
    The initial opening screen appears as shown in Figure 5.7.

Figure 5.7

Loading the
MemMaker
program.

```
Microsoft MemMaker
_____

Welcome to MemMaker.

MemMaker optimizes your system's memory by moving memory-resident
programs and device drivers into the upper memory area. This
frees conventional memory for use by applications.

After you run MemMaker, your computer's memory will remain
optimized until you add or remove memory-resident programs or
device drivers. For an optimum memory configuration, run MemMaker
again after making any such changes.

MemMaker displays options as highlighted text. (For example, you
can change the "Continue" option below.) To cycle through the
available options, press SPACEBAR. When MemMaker displays the
option you want, press ENTER.

For help while you are running MemMaker, press F1.

                   Continue or Exit? Continue

ENTER=Accept Selection   SPACEBAR=Change Selection   F1=Help   F3=Exit
```

b. To proceed with the memory optimization:
    PRESS: (Enter)
    The following screen appears (Figure 5.8) asking you to select between
    an Express or Custom setup. (*Note*: You should use the Custom setup
    only if you are very experienced at modifying your computer's
    CONFIG.SYS and AUTOEXEC.BAT commands.)

Figure 5.8

Choosing an
optimization
method in
MemMaker.

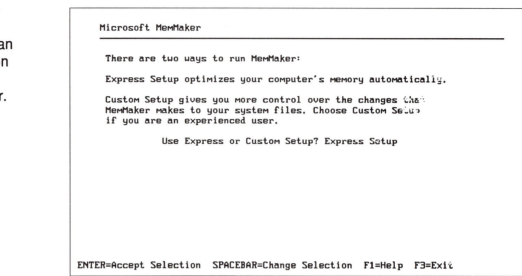

```
Microsoft MemMaker

  There are two ways to run MemMaker:

  Express Setup optimizes your computer's memory automatically.

  Custom Setup gives you more control over the changes that
  MemMaker makes to your system files. Choose Custom Setup
  if you are an experienced user.

            Use Express or Custom Setup? Express Setup




  ENTER=Accept Selection   SPACEBAR=Change Selection   F1=Help   F3=Exit
```

   c. SELECT: Express option
       PRESS: ⌈Enter⌋
       If you wanted to use the Custom option, you would press the Space
       Bar to cycle through the available choices and then press ⌈Enter⌋.
       Figure 5.9 shows the next selection screen where MemMaker asks you
       whether your application software programs require expanded memory
       (EMS). (*Note*: Not many application programs require EMS.)

Figure 5.9

Choosing
between EMS
and non-EMS
support for
applications.

```
Microsoft MemMaker
─────────────────────────────────────────────────────────────────────

If you use any programs that require expanded memory (EMS), answer
Yes to the following question.  Answering Yes makes expanded memory
available, but might not free as much conventional memory.

If none of your programs need expanded memory, answer No to the
following question.  Answering No makes expanded memory unavailable,
but can free more conventional memory.

If you are not sure whether your programs require expanded memory,
answer No.  If you later discover that a program needs expanded
memory, run MemMaker again and answer Yes to this question.

Do you use any programs that need expanded memory (EMS)? No




ENTER=Accept Selection   SPACEBAR=Change Selection   F1=Help   F3=Exit
```

    d. SELECT: No EMS
       PRESS: [Enter]

Once you have completed these steps, MemMaker reboots the computer,
analyzes your computer's customization files, makes the necessary changes,
and then reboots the computer a second time. This second rebooting is a
test of the changes made to the customization files. If all goes well, you
will be asked to accept the changes before exiting MemMaker. If your
computer does not reboot successfully, you may need to bypass the
CONFIG.SYS and AUTOEXEC.BAT files during the startup process by
pressing [F5]. When the system prompt appears, you enter the command
MEMMAKER /UNDO to reverse the changes made to these files and then
reboot the computer a final time.

Quick Reference	Command:	MEMMAKER (external)
MEMMAKER	Syntax:	memmaker [/batch or /undo]
Command	Purpose:	Automatically configures your computer to optimize RAM

DISPLAYING TECHNICAL INFORMATION (MSD)

The Microsoft Diagnostics program was first included with Windows 3.1 to assist Microsoft support personnel responding to users with hardware and software conflicts. Since most people are not well educated on the innards of their computer system, the support personnel ask users to run this program to display such technical details as the processor type, operating system version, and video card manufacturer of their computer. Microsoft now includes this useful diagnostics program with DOS 6.

You load Microsoft Diagnostics by typing MSD at the system prompt and pressing (Enter). Perform the following steps:

1. To load Microsoft Diagnostics:
    TYPE: msd
    PRESS: (Enter)
    Your screen should appear similar to Figure 5.10.

Figure 5.10

Displaying system information using the MSD command.

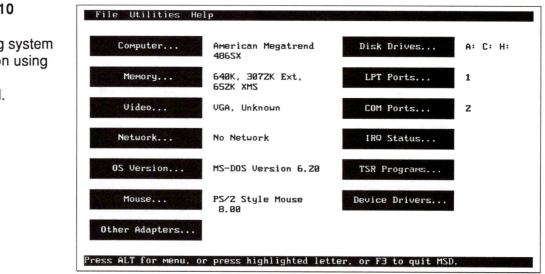

2. For further details about your system, you select a category button:
    CHOOSE: Computer button

3. To return to the main screen:
    PRESS: (Enter) or CLICK: OK

4. To print a report of your computer's technical specifications:
   CHOOSE: File, Print Report
   The following screen appears, as shown in Figure 5.11.

Figure 5.11

Printing a report
from Microsoft
Diagnostics.

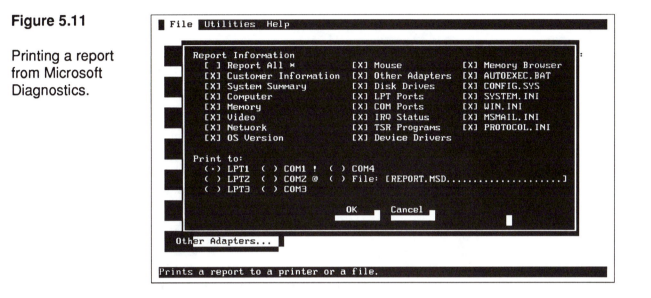

5. For a complete report:
   SELECT: Report All * (in the Report Information area)

6. Since the report can sometimes exceed 20 pages, let's send it to a file
   on the Advantage Diskette rather than the printer:
   SELECT: File (in the Print to area)

7. Enter a new file name for the report:
   TYPE: a:\msdinfo.txt
   PRESS: (Enter) or CLICK: OK

8. Complete the Customer Information dialog box that appears by typing
   in text and pressing (Tab) to move to the next field or blank. When you
   have completed filling in the dialog box, press (Enter) to proceed. The
   file is saved to the Advantage Diskette in drive A:. In the next section,
   you will use the MORE command to view the file.

9. CHOOSE: File, Exit

Quick Reference   Command: MSD (external)
MSD Command   Syntax: msd
                       Purpose: Displays technical information about your computer

---

MISCELLANEOUS COMMANDS

This section introduces the DOS redirection symbols for changing the standard input and output devices. You also learn to use the MORE and XCOPY commands, which offer enhanced versions of TYPE and COPY. For protecting your computer system, you are introduced to a new feature of DOS 6 called the Microsoft Anti-Virus program.

REDIRECTING INPUT AND OUTPUT

DOS provides a method for redirecting the input sources and output destinations for a command. For example, the standard input device is the keyboard. However, you can also feed data to a command from a file or a modem communications line. For the output of a command, the screen is the standard device. With redirection symbols, you can send the output from a command to a file or the printer instead. This technique is especially useful for saving the contents of a directory listing in a file or producing a disk or memory status report using CHKDSK or MEM. Table 5.5 contains the DOS redirection symbols.

Table 5.5	*Symbol*	*Description*
Redirection Symbols	<	Input redirection symbol; accepts input from a source other than the keyboard
	>	Output redirection symbol; sends output to a destination other than the screen

Table 5.5 (continued)	*Symbol*	*Description*
	>>	Append redirection symbol; appends output to an existing file
	|	Pipe symbol; allows the output of one command to become the input for another command

The best way to understand redirection is to use it in some examples. Perform the following steps.

1. Ensure that the Advantage Diskette is placed into drive A:, the A:\> system prompt is displayed, and that your printer is on-line and ready.

2. To save a list of the directory contents for the Advantage Diskette:
   TYPE: `dir > dirlist.txt`
   PRESS: (Enter)
   Notice that there are several parts to this command. First, the DIR command is entered using the normal syntax to produce a directory listing. A space separates the command from the output redirection symbol (>). Another space separates the symbol from the target or destination. Lastly, the destination for the listing is a disk file called DIRLIST.TXT.

   CAUTION: You do not need to enter a space between the redirection symbol and the other parameters. However, we recommend that you always place a space after a DOS command and between parameters.

3. To view the file DIRLIST.TXT:
   TYPE: `type dirlist.txt`
   PRESS: (Enter)
   The contents of DIRLIST.TXT scroll onto the screen.

4. To append a new view of the directory to the same file:
   TYPE: `dir /w >> dirlist.txt`
   PRESS: (Enter)
   Notice that the >> or Append redirection symbol separates the command from the destination.

5. To send the contents of the file DIRLIST.TXT to the printer:
    TYPE: `type dirlist.txt > prn`
    PRESS: Enter
    In this step, the > symbol redirects the output to the default printer device called PRN.

Quick Reference
Using Redirection Symbols

Use the following redirection symbols to change the standard input (keyboard) and output (screen) devices:
<   Input redirection symbol
>   Output redirection symbol
>> Append redirection symbol
| Pipe symbol

VIEWING THE CONTENTS OF A FILE (MORE)

The MORE command displays an ASCII text file on the screen. Unlike the TYPE command, MORE allows you to leisurely view a text file one screen at a time. When one screen is filled with information, the scrolling stops and the message "-- MORE --" appears in the bottom left-hand corner of the screen. Press the Space Bar to view the next screen of information.

The syntax for the MORE command follows:

MORE < *file name*, or
commandname | MORE

The MORE command uses the input redirection symbol to feed data to the command. Alternatively, you place the MORE command after another command using the pipe symbol (|). This keeps the first command's output from scrolling too quickly on the screen. For example, if you perform a DIR command in a directory containing hundreds of files, the information scrolls by on the screen very quickly. Rather than using the /P switch with DIR, you could enter DIR | MORE to produce the same result.

To illustrate the MORE command, perform the following steps at the A:\> system prompt.

1. To list the contents of the MSDINFO.TXT file:
    TYPE: `type msdinfo.txt`
    PRESS: Enter

2. To list the contents of MSDINFO.TXT one screen at a time:
   TYPE: `more < msdinfo.txt`
   PRESS: (Enter)

3. PRESS: Space Bar repeatedly until the system prompt appears

4. To perform a directory of the Advantage Diskette:
   TYPE: `dir | more`
   PRESS: (Enter)

5. PRESS: Space Bar to continue

....

Quick Reference *MORE Command*	Command:	MORE (external)
	Syntax:	more < *file name*, or *commandname* | more
	Purpose:	Displays output of a command one screen at a time

....

COPYING FILES AND DIRECTORIES (XCOPY)

The XCOPY command is an enhanced version of COPY. Not only does XCOPY copy files, it copies entire directory trees. This command works extremely well for moving a branch of subdirectories from one disk drive to another. The syntax for the XCOPY command follows:

XCOPY *source destination* [/A] [/D:*date*] [/E] [/M] [/P] [/S] [/V]

/A	Copies files with the archive file attribute; keeps attribute
/D:*date*	Copies files created on or after the specified date, for example, `xcopy *.xls a:\data /d:6/30/94`
/E	Creates subdirectories for the target even if empty
/M	Copies files with the archive file attribute; removes attribute
/P	Prompts you before overwriting a file
/S	Copies subdirectories and files
/V	Verifies that each copy is complete and accurate

Perform the following steps.

1. Ensure that the A:\> system prompt is displayed.

2. To create a sample directory structure:
    TYPE: md \workdata
    PRESS: [Enter]
    TYPE: md \workdata\budgets
    PRESS: [Enter]
    TYPE: md \workdata\invoices
    PRESS: [Enter]
    TYPE: md \homedata
    PRESS: [Enter]

3. To copy the files without an extension from the root directory to the BUDGETS directory:
    TYPE: xcopy *. \workdata\budgets
    PRESS: [Enter]
    The files are read into memory and then copied to the \WORKDATA\BUDGETS directory.

4. To copy the TXT files from the root directory to the INVOICES directory:
    TYPE: xcopy *.txt \workdata\invoices
    PRESS: [Enter]

5. To copy everything under the \WORKDATA directory to the \HOMEDATA directory:
    TYPE: xcopy \workdata \homedata /s
    PRESS: [Enter]

6. TYPE: dir \homedata
    PRESS: [Enter]
    Notice that the two subdirectories, BUDGETS and INVOICES, now appear under the HOMEDATA directory as well.

7. Clear the screen.

....

Quick Reference   Command: XCOPY (external)
XCOPY Command   Syntax: xcopy *source destination* [/a] [/d:*date*] [/e] [/m] [/p] [/s] [/v]
                      Purpose: Copies files and directories

....

PROTECTING AGAINST VIRUSES (MSAV)

Viruses are malicious programs created to wreak havoc on unsuspecting computer users. Some **viruses** just surprise you with harmless messages or system sounds, while others can wipe out your entire hard disk. In DOS 6, Microsoft provides a program called Microsoft Anti-Virus (available for both DOS and Windows environments) to protect your computer system from these unwanted critters. You load Microsoft Anti-Virus by typing MSAV and pressing (Enter).

Perform the following steps.

1. Ensure that the A:\> system prompt is displayed.

2. To load Microsoft Anti-Virus:
   TYPE: msav
   PRESS: (Enter)
   The screen shown in Figure 5.12 appears.

Figure 5.12

Loading Microsoft
Anti-Virus.

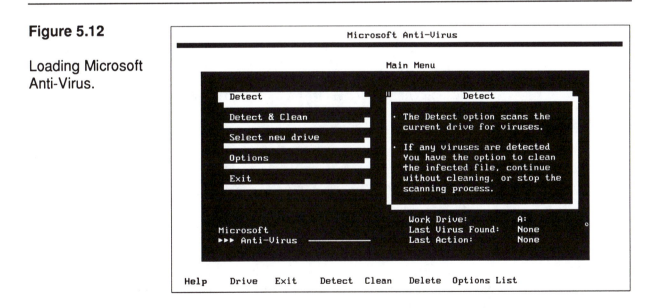

3. To destroy any viruses found on drive A:, do the following:
   CHOOSE: Detect & Clean command button
   Once Microsoft Anti-Virus completes the scan of the Advantage Diskette, a summary dialog box appears as shown in Figure 5.13.

Figure 5.13

Displaying the
results of a virus
scan.

```
┌──────────────────────────────────────────────────────────────┐
│                      Microsoft Anti-Virus                      │
│  ════════════════════════════════════════════════════════════  │
│                           Main Menu                            │
│                  Viruses Detected and Cleaned                  │
│                                                                │
│                      Checked      Infected      Cleaned        │
│                                                                │
│       Hard disks   :     0           0             0           │
│       Floppy disks :     1           0             0           │
│       Total disks  :     1           0             0           │
│                                                                │
│       COM Files    :     0           0             0           │
│       EXE Files    :     0           0             0           │
│       Other Files  :    58           0             0           │
│       Total Files  :    58           0             0           │
│                                                                │
│       Scan Time    :   00:00:20                                │
│                                                                │
│                                                                │
│  ─────────────────────────────────────────────────────────    │
│                                                                │
│   Stop                                                         │
└──────────────────────────────────────────────────────────────┘
```

4. To proceed, do the following:
    PRESS: Enter or CLICK: OK
    CHOOSE: Exit command button

5. Respond negatively to any prompts asking you to save your choices.

....

Quick Reference   Command: MSAV (external)
MSAV Command   Syntax: msav
                       Purpose: Detects and cleans viruses found on your computer

....

SUMMARY

This session introduced you to the DOS Editor for creating ASCII text
files. A great improvement over the EDLIN line editor, the new DOS
Editor is used to create, save, and print batch files, system files, and other
text files. You also gained experience creating DOSKEY macros and batch
files, which are text files used for automating frequently performed file and
disk management tasks.

The session also discussed the different types of memory and presented a new program in DOS 6, called MemMaker, for optimizing your computer's memory. Another new feature introduced this session is the Microsoft Anti-Virus program, a protection scheme designed to detect and destroy viruses that may be harmful to your computer system. In addition to some miscellaneous commands, this session introduced the redirection symbols, which allow you to specify alternative input and output devices. Rather than sending output to the screen, you can easily redirect it to the printer or a disk file. Many of the commands and procedures appearing in this session are provided in Table 5.6, the Command Summary.

Table 5.6	*Command*	*Description*
Command Summary	EDIT	Loads the DOS Editor for creating and saving text files
	DOSKEY	Recalls and edits DOS commands, and creates macros
	MEM	Displays memory information for your computer
	MEMMAKER	Automatically configures your computer to optimize conventional memory (RAM)
	MSD	Displays technical information about your computer
	MORE	Displays output of a text file one screen at a time
	XCOPY	Copies files and directories
	MSAV	Detects and cleans viruses found on your computer
DOS Editor Commands	File, Save	Saves a file to the disk under the current file name
	File, Save As	Saves a file to the disk under a new name
	File, Open	Opens an existing file
	File, Print	Prints a selected area of text or the entire document
	File, Exit	Leaves the DOS Editor program

KEY TERMS

batch file   A text file containing DOS commands; used to perform frequent or repetitive tasks. Every batch file has an extension of BAT.

conventional memory   The area from 0 KB to 640 KB in RAM.

expanded memory   Additional memory, usually provided by an add-in memory board; extended memory can emulate expanded memory.

extended memory   The area above 1 MB in RAM.

High Memory Area (HMA)   The first 64 KB block of extended memory. DOS loads some of the operating system code into this area.

macro   A collection of DOS commands stored in RAM. Similar in principle to a batch file, a macro is stored in the computer's memory and executes much faster than commands in a batch file.

RAM   Random access memory; volatile memory that provides the work area for most programs and data. RAM is divided into conventional, extended, and expanded memory.

ROM   Read-only memory that contains instructions for the basic input and output operations of the computer.

upper memory   Reserved memory area for hardware devices, such as a graphics adapter; the area located between 640 KB and 1 MB.

viruses   Programs designed with a malicious intent to display messages, produce sounds, damage files and disks, and generally corrupt your computer system.

EXERCISES

SHORT ANSWER

1. Name three types of files that you can create using the DOS Editor.
2. What information is provided in the bottom right-hand corner of the Editor screen?

3. Why should you avoid naming a batch file after an existing DOS command?
4. What is the purpose of the REM batch subcommand?
5. What are the two primary functions of the DOSKEY command?
6. What is the main difference between a macro and a batch file?
7. How can you save macros so that you do not have to enter them each time you boot the computer?
8. What are the standard input and output devices? Name some alternatives to these standard devices.
9. When would you use the XCOPY command instead of COPY?
10. Name the different memory areas and their capacities on a computer with 4 MB RAM.

HANDS-ON

(*Note*: In the following exercises, you perform DOS commands using files located on the Advantage Diskette.)

1. The objective of the first exercise is to create a batch file using the DOS Editor program. Once it's created, you execute the program from the command line.
   a. Ensure that the A:\> system prompt is displayed.
   b. Create a simple batch file program called TYPEOUT.BAT:
      TYPE: `edit typeout.bat`
      PRESS: [Enter]
   c. Enter the following lines into the batch file:

      ```
      cls
      type example.txt
      cls
      type hardware.txt
      ```

   d. Save the file and exit the DOS Editor.
   e. Execute the TYPEOUT.BAT batch file:
      TYPE: `typeout`
      PRESS: [Enter]
      Notice that once the EXAMPLE.TXT file appears, the screen is cleared and the HARDWARE.TXT file is displayed.
   f. In the next several steps you will edit the batch file to include pauses after the first TYPE command and to turn off the display of the commands:
      TYPE: `edit typeout.bat`
      PRESS: [Enter]

g. Use the ECHO OFF batch subcommand to turn off the display of commands to the screen:
TYPE: `echo off`
PRESS: (Enter)
Notice that the CLS command is moved to the second line.

h. Position the cursor underneath the letter "c" in the second CLS command.

i. Insert a pause in the batch file after the first TYPE command:
TYPE: `pause`
PRESS: (Enter)
Your screen should now appear similar to Figure 5.14.

Figure 5.14

TYPEOUT.BAT
batch file.

```
 File  Edit  Search  Options                                   Help
                            TYPEOUT.BAT
echo off
cls
type example.txt
pause
cls
type hardware.txt




MS-DOS Editor  <F1=Help> Press ALT to activate menus          00005:001
```

j. Save the file and exit the DOS Editor.

k. Execute the TYPEOUT batch file. Notice that the batch file executes with a much cleaner screen using the ECHO OFF command. After the first file is typed to the screen, the batch file pauses for a keystroke. Strike the Space Bar to proceed with typing the HARDWARE.TXT file.

2. In this exercise, you practice using the DOSKEY command to create macro commands. You also use the redirection symbol to create a batch file that automatically loads the macros.

a. Ensure that the A:\> system prompt is displayed.

b. Load the DOSKEY program.

c. Enter the following commands:

```
dir /w
cls
ver
dir /os /p
cls
chkdsk
```

d. View the list of commands stored by the DOSKEY command.

e. Create a macro called SENDEX that lists the EXAMPLE.TXT file to the screen.
TYPE: `doskey sendex=type example.txt`
PRESS: [Enter]

f. Perform the SENDEX macro:
TYPE: `sendex`
PRESS: [Enter]

g. Create a macro called SENDHW that lists the HARDWARE.TXT file to the screen.
TYPE: `doskey sendhw=type hardware.txt`
PRESS: [Enter]

h. Perform the SENDHW macro.

i. View the list of macros stored by the DOSKEY command.

j. Create a batch file called SENDMACS.BAT that automatically loads these macros:
TYPE: `doskey /macros > sendmacs.bat`
PRESS: [Enter]

k. Load the SENDMACS.BAT file in the DOS Editor:
TYPE: `edit sendmacs.bat`
PRESS: [Enter]

l. At the beginning of each line, insert the DOSKEY command. Your screen should now appear similar to Figure 5.15.

Figure 5.15

SENDMACS.BAT
batch file.

```
 File  Edit  Search  Options                                        Help
                        SENDMACS.BAT
doskey SENDEX=type example.txt
doskey SENDHW=type hardware.txt




















MS-DOS Editor  <F1=Help> Press ALT to activate menus            00002:008
```

     m. Save the file and exit the DOS Editor.

     n. Reinstall a new copy of the DOSKEY command.
        TYPE: `doskey /reinstall`
        PRESS: (Enter)

     o. Load the macros using the SENDMACS.BAT file:
        TYPE: `sendmacs`
        PRESS: (Enter)
        The macros are automatically loaded into memory.

3. For this exercise, you create two text files and then combine them using the redirection symbols.

     a. Ensure that the A:\> system prompt is displayed.

     b. Create a text file called CHAPTER1:
        TYPE: `edit chapter1`
        PRESS: (Enter)

     c. Enter the following text:

```
Chapter 1: Tennis
I. Equipment
      a. Racket
      b. Shoes
      c. Clothing
II. Conditioning
      a. Aerobic
      b. Anaerobic
```

```
III. Groundstrokes
       a. Forehand
       b. Backhand
IV. Service
       a. Flat
       b. Slice
       c. American Twist
V. Net Play
       a. Volley
       b. Smash
VI. Strategy and Rules
```

d. Save the file.
e. Create a new file called CHAPTER2:
   CHOOSE: File, New
f. Enter the following text:

```
Chapter 2: Golf
I. Equipment
       a. Woods
       b. Irons
       c. Shoes
       d. Glove
II. From the Tee
       a. Wood
       b. Iron
III. From the Fairway
       a. Wood
       b. Iron >150 yards
       c. Iron <150 yards
IV. Approach
       a. 100 yards
       b. 80 yards
       c. 60 yards
V. Chip
       a. Fringe
       b. Trap
VI. Putting
```

g. Save the file as CHAPTER2.
h. Exit the DOS Editor.
i. List CHAPTER1 to the screen:
   TYPE: type chapter1
   PRESS: [Enter]
j. List CHAPTER2 to the screen:
   TYPE: type chapter2
   PRESS: [Enter]

k. Save the listing to a new file called BOOK:
    TYPE: `type chapter1 > book`
    PRESS: Enter
l. Add CHAPTER2 to the new file:
    TYPE: `type chapter2 >> book`
    PRESS: Enter
m. List the new file one screen at a time:
    TYPE: `more < book`
    PRESS: Enter
    PRESS: Space Bar when prompted

DOS 6:
COMMAND-LINE SUMMARY

Command	Syntax	Description
ATTRIB	attrib [+/-] [r] [a] [s] [h] *file name*	Views and changes the attributes of one or more files
CD	cd *pathname*	Changes to another directory
CHKDSK	chkdsk [*drive:*] [/f] [/v]	Checks and verifies the readability of a disk, and corrects file system errors
CLS	cls	Clears the screen
COPY	copy *source destination*	Makes a duplicate of one or more files
DATE	date [*mm-dd-yy*]	Sets the date for the system clock
DBLSPACE	dblspace	Compresses the files on a disk to increase its capacity
DEFRAG	defrag [*drive:*] [/f or /u] [/b] [/v]	Optimizes a disk by defragmenting its files
DEL	del *file specification*	Deletes one or more files
DELTREE	deltree *pathname* [*pathname1*] [...]	Removes a branch of subdirectories and files
DIR	dir [*drive:*] [/p] [/w] [/o[-][n,e,s,d]] [/a[-][r,a,s,h]]	Lists the files stored on a disk or in a directory
DISKCOPY	diskcopy *source destination* [/v]	Duplicates an entire diskette
DOSKEY	doskey [/reinstall] [/macros] [/history] [*macroname=[commands]*]	Recalls and edits DOS commands, and creates command-line macros
EDIT	edit [*file name*]	Loads the DOS Editor for creating and saving text files
FORMAT	format [*drive:*] [/q] [/u] [/f:*size*] [/s] [/v:*label*]	Prepares or initializes a disk for storage
HELP	help *command* (or *command* /?)	Provides help for a DOS command
LABEL	label [*drive:*] [*name*]	Creates, changes, and deletes a drive's volume label
MD	md *pathname*	Makes a new directory
MEM	mem [/c] [/d] [/p]	Displays memory information for your computer
MEMMAKER	memmaker [/batch or /undo]	Automatically configures your computer to optimize RAM
MORE	more < *file name* or *command*	more	Displays output of a text file or command one screen at a time
MOVE	move *source destination*	Moves one or more files to a different drive or directory, and renames directories
MSAV	msav	Detects and cleans viruses found on your computer

Command	Syntax	Description
MSBACKUP	msbackup [*setup file*]	Backs up and restores your hard disk files
MSD	msd	Displays technical information about your computer
PATH	path *pathname1* [;*pathname2*;...]	Displays or sets the search path for program files
PROMPT	prompt pg	Changes the DOS system prompt for the command line
RD	rd *pathname*	Removes a directory
REN	ren *oldname newname*	Changes the name of one or more files
SCANDISK	scandisk [*drive:* or /all]	Analyzes and corrects problems with disks
TIME	time [*hh:mm*]	Sets the time for the system clock
TREE	tree [*drive:*] [/a] [/f]	Displays a graphical view of a directory structure
TYPE	type *file name*	Views the contents of an ASCII text file
UNDELETE	undelete [/unload] [/s[*drive*]] [/t*drive*] undelete [*file spec.*] [/all] [/list]	Sets up the Undelete program's level of protection and restores one or more files
UNFORMAT	unformat *drive:* [/l] [/test]	Restores an accidentally formatted disk
VER	ver	Displays the DOS version number
VOL	vol [*drive:*]	Displays a drive's volume label and serial number
XCOPY	xcopy *source destination* [/a] [/d:*date*] [/e] [/m] [/p] [/s] [/v]	Copies files and subdirectories

INDEX

DOS 6